# CANTERBUR

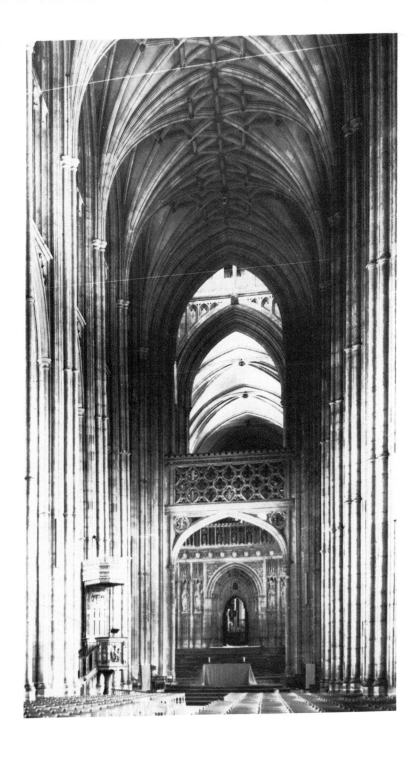

*The New Bell's Cathedral Guides*

# CANTERBURY CATHEDRAL

THE REVEREND CANON D. INGRAM HILL

PHOTOGRAPHY BY PETER BURTON
AND HARLAND WALSHAW

First published 1986 by
Bell & Hyman Limited
Denmark House
37–39 Queen Elizabeth Street
London SE1 2QB

Designed by Colin Lewis

**British Library Cataloguing in Publication Data**
    Ingram Hill, D.
      Canterbury Cathedral. — (The new Bell's cathedral guides)
      1.   Canterbury Cathedral — Guide-books
      2.   Canterbury (Kent) — Churches
      I.   Title
      914.22'22'34     DA690.C3

ISBN 0-7135-2619-X (paperback)
ISBN 0-7135-2618-1 (cased)

Typeset by Typecast Ltd., Maidstone
Printed in Great Britain at the University Press, Cambridge

# CONTENTS

*Chapter One*

# A HISTORY OF THE CATHEDRAL

T HE GREAT EAST window of the cathedral Chapter House depicts twenty-one outstanding personalities in the long history of the cathedral. The series ends with Queen Victoria, who was celebrating her Diamond Jubilee in 1897, shortly before the glass was inserted and begins, appropriately enough, with the sixth-century Queen Bertha, who might be called the founding mother of both the cathedral and the Church in England. The great west window shows the founding of Canterbury as the religious centre of England: Augustine meeting Queen Bertha and her husband Ethelbert King of Kent after his landing at Ebbsfleet on the Kent coast; Augustine preaching the Gospel to them and their court; and the baptism of the pagan King Ethelbert in the font of St Martin's Church on the outskirts of Canterbury.

The baptism, which traditionally took place on Whitsunday AD 597 was followed by an act of generosity on the part of the king, who handed over his palace and the surrounding grounds to the monk-missionaries as a base of operations from which they could preach and baptize across his kingdom. The king himself moved his seat of government to Reculver, a few miles away on the coast. Near the palace were the ruins of a Christian Church of Romano-British origin in use before the withdrawal of the Roman armies *c.* AD 410, which was to become the first cathedral, known in subsequent centuries either as St Saviour's, the Holy Trinity, or more usually as Christ Church as it is known today. This building, which may well have been a basilica or law court attached to the Roman Governor's Palace before its conversion into a Christian Church, would have been situated in an area now occupied by the Cathedral Precincts. According to the Venerable Bede, Augustine would have placed his episcopal 'cathedra' or official seat of office in this church, in accordance with traditional Roman practice, after his consecration by bishops of the Church in Gaul at Arles. For three and a half centuries the first Saxon archbishops, including the eminent scholar Theodore of Tarsus, officiated here and left on their tours of the diocese and province of Canterbury.

It was during the primacy of St Odo (942-958) that a major restoration of the building took place. He is recorded as raising the walls by twenty feet (six metres), which would have allowed for the insertion of a clerestory. The work which Odo undertook was inspired by a visit to Rome and it is thought that he intended to remodel his cathedral on the lines of the great basilicas he had seen there. Since the work took five years, it must have been on a large scale and the building, when finished, had two towers on each side dedicated to St Gregory on the south and St Martin on the north. The altar was in an apse constructed of great stones and mortar against the east wall with a crypt underneath the sanctuary area, and another altar stood a little to the west for the daily celebration of the Eucharist. Here in 988 the greatest of all the archbishops of the late Saxon centuries, St Dunstan, was buried.

In 1011 catastrophe fell upon the cathedral and the Archbishop, the saintly monk Alphege, when the city was besieged by the Danes, captured and sacked. The cathedral was set on fire causing much damage, while the Archbishop was carried off to the Danish camp at Greenwich and eventually martyred by his enraged captors. Reacting to this crime with revulsion, the Danish King Canute repaired the damaged cathedral after his own conversion, and buried the martyr's body within it. As an act of reparation, the king gave the cathedral and its monks 'his crown of gold, which is still kept at the head of the great cross or rood in the nave'.

The Saxon monk, Eadmer, who is our authority for this, goes on to tell of another disaster which struck the cathedral only a few years after these repairs. In 1067, a year after the Norman conquest, when Archbishop Stigand was deprived of his position and imprisoned by William the Conqueror, fire broke out in the cathedral and consumed the whole building. When Lanfranc, the Conqueror's trusted adviser and friend, came from Caen to be consecrated as the new archbishop of Canterbury in 1070, the ceremony had to take place in a shed among the ruins.

Though an elderly man by the standards of that time, Lanfranc tackled the immense problems confronting him with tremendous energy. In the midst of successful attempts to reform and revitalize the Church in England he found time to superintend the building of a great church which was at once to serve the needs of a growing

Benedictine community and also to be the cathedral church of the diocese and a model to the whole province of which he was now primate. The construction work took seven years. It appears to have borne a strong resemblance to the abbey church of St Etienne in Caen of which Lanfranc had been abbot: the nave terminated in two western towers, and the small sanctuary was raised on a crypt and consisted of only two bays with an apse. At the end of the nave was a lantern tower with a pyramidal top which was later surmounted by the figure of an angel, causing it to be known as the Angel Steeple. The north-west tower survived for seven hundred and fifty years until its demolition c. 1834.

Impressive as this church must have seemed at its completion in 1077 when the monks took possession of it, with the arrival of Lanfranc's successor, Anselm, from the Abbey of Bec in 1093 it was soon clear that it was too small for the growing number of monks in the community to offer their daily round of liturgical worship with appropriate dignity. This was the golden age of the Benedictine Order and Anselm's pre-eminence in learning and sanctity drew men to him and to the community at Canterbury from all over Europe. Despite his long absence abroad as a result of the conflict between Church and State over Investitures, the work of the extension of the cathedral to the east was begun in 1096 and finally consecrated in 1130, long after Anselm's death in 1109. Christ Church was fortunate in having at the head of its monks two great priors at this vital time in its history to supervise the building work: Ernulf, who took office in the year when the great extension was begun; and Conrad who succeeded him in 1114 on his departure to become Abbot of Peterborough.

As a cathedral, Christ Church can have had few equals in Europe at the time of its consecration. At the east end of Lanfranc's imposing nave was a screen surmounted by a great cross or rood with figures of angels as well as those of St Mary and St John. Then came the vast crypt which remains today one of the most impressive Romanesque structures in existence. This has an aisled nave, processional aisles on each side of the main crypt, and transepts each with two apsidal chapels, as well as the eastern chapels of Holy Innocents and St Gabriel. These were ornamented and adorned with rich carvings on pillars and arcades and also splendid paintings on the walls and vaulting.

Above this crypt was erected the huge choir for the monks. Here are eastern transepts as in the undercroft below, each with its two apsidal chapels and, at the east end behind the High Altar and Sanctuary, an ambulatory with the Altar of the Holy Trinity where St

Romanesque pillars in the western crypt.

The 'Sedes Marmorea' or Marble Chair of the Primates behind the High Altar.

Thomas was to say his first mass as a priest in 1162. This great extension was nine bays in length with an apsidal sanctuary of seven bays. The Romanesque arcading which runs round this part of the church both inside and outside the exterior walls can still be seen, together with two of the small spiked towers (originally six in number) which were an unusual feature of the exterior of this great building. Two side chapels also survive, dedicated to St Andrew, and St Peter and St Paul respectively, and were entered from the eastern ambulatory. A great wooden vault similar to that at the contemporaneous Ely Cathedral stretched over the Romanesque Choir of Canterbury. Behind the High Altar stood the 'Sedes Marmorea', the ancient name for the Patriarchal Chair of the Primates, and over the altar was a great beam from which hung a pyx containing the Reserved Sacrament and on which were caskets of relics. At right angles to this were placed subsidiary altars where the relics of St Alphege and St Dunstan were enshrined.

The great new choir was dedicated in a ceremony described by the monastic chronicler Gervase: 'so famous a dedication has never been heard of on earth since the dedication of the Temple of Solomon'. Archbishop de Corbeuil presided while King Henry I and King David of Scotland headed the contingent of lay folk. Also present were eight

9

*The Norman Water Tower built under the direction of Prior Wibert.*

bishops of the province of Canterbury, three foreign bishops and many other clergy.

Prior Conrad had died four years before this ceremony, and his successors for the next thirty years were monks who have left no great mark on the history of their community. In 1153 another great builder, Wibert, became prior, remembered for his notable additions to the domestic buildings of the priory. He was fortunate in having as archbishop Theobold, a monk of Bec, who restored the depleted finances of the house to stability, thus enabling his prior to embark on many projects which are still with us today. These may well include the carving of the crypt capitals and the painting of St Gabriel's and St Anselm's Chapels. Most important were the building of the Vestiarium or Treasury; the Cemetery Gate, now the entrance to the Kent War Memorial Garden in the Precincts; the fine gate of the Green Court, to which Prior Chillenden added an upper storey two hundred years later; and the grand Norman staircase next door. Not least among his improvements was the famous water system which bears his name and which is still at work, represented visually by the lovely Water Tower which can be seen across the Green Court on the north side of the Precincts.

By the end of Wibert's term of office, the buildings of the priory as well as the great cathedral church were complete. The full life of a Benedictine monk, in accordance with the Rule of St Benedict and the Monastic Constitutions drawn up by Lanfranc, was being lived out in all its minute detail of ceremonial and liturgy. Despite the impact of political events, controversies and conflagrations, it continued thus for nearly four centuries until the Dissolution.

Wibert died in 1167, and so would have been in office at Theobald's death and at the consecration of his successor, Thomas Becket. Perhaps fortunately for him, another monk, Odo, was prior at the time of the murder.

After his enthronement, Becket's contact with his cathedral and its monastery was slight, for he was very soon involved in the famous and ultimately fatal quarrel with Henry II over the treatment of criminous clerks and those clauses to which he objected in the Constitutions of Clarendon. In these Henry set forth the customs in force in England in the time of his grandfather Henry I, when the controversy with Anselm took place. This quarrel drove Becket into exile in 1164 for six years.

Canterbury comes back into the picture on 2 December 1170, when Becket made his triumphant progress from Sandwich, where he had landed after his voyage across the Channel from the French port of Wissant. Everywhere as he passed through the villages along the road from the coast, he was greeted by cheering crowds, delighted to have their Father in God in their midst again. The Archbishop is recorded as being depressed and full of foreboding of tragedy to come. His sermon in the cathedral on Christmas morning ended with the pronouncement of excommunication against all those who had been the means of his falling out with the King which included Roger, the Archbishop of York, who had presumed to crown the 'Young King' Henry in Becket's absence. To him he added the Bishops of London and Salisbury, and other of his enemies.

The rage of Henry II at Becket's doings after his return provoked him to those famous and ill-considered words: 'Will none of you rid me of this turbulent priest?' From the castle of Burs near Bayeux, where Henry had

*The door leading from the Archbishop's Palace to the cloister.*

been spending Christmas, the four knights who were to be Becket's murderers rode fast to the coast and arrived at the Palace of Canterbury on 29 December. After a furious altercation with the Archbishop in his hall they withdrew to arm themselves, to find on their return that his terrified attendants had almost bodily carried their master out of a side door around the cloister to the cathedral. They entered, as was customary, by the door that still leads from the cloister into the north-west transept. Becket might easily have saved himself in the recesses of the great Romanesque church, which in the late afternoon was dark, for the monks were just beginning Vespers, but he had insisted on the cloister door being left open behind him. On the pavement before the altar of St Benedict, just inside the door, his enemies killed him, leaving his corpse lying on the floor before the altar. The contemporary chronicler, Garnier de Sainte-Maxence, describes the last moments vividly: 'Now indeed St Thomas saw his martyrdom approaching. Hands joined before his face, he gave himself to the Lord God commending himself, his cause and the cause of the holy church to the martyr St Denis, to whom sweet France belongs, and to the saints of the church.' The chronicler ends his account with words which inspired medieval poets and preachers in their panegyrics of St Thomas: 'Anyone who saw the blood and the brains fall and lie mingled on the stone floor might have thought of roses and lilies.'

After the murder, when they recovered from the shock and horror, the monks took up the dead body of the martyred prelate and prepared it for burial. After the body had lain in state before the High Altar, the monks carried it in solemn procession to the crypt below and buried it there at the east end behind the altar of Our Lady in a hastily prepared tomb. It was here that Henry II came on 12 July 1174 to perform his penance, being scourged by eighty monks, each laying on three strokes, and then fasting at the tomb until the morning. Then, absolved, and no doubt much relieved to be at peace with his dead adversary, he rode away.

Any exultation that the monks of the priory may have felt at this singular episode in church history was soon wiped out by a disaster which fell upon the cathedral only eight weeks later. At about 3 pm on 5 September fire broke out in a cottage in Burgate Street. The south wind carried sparks across the Precincts to the roof of the great choir, where they appear to have lodged in the joints of the lead roof and ignited the wooden rafters below. Despite the efforts of the monks and some of the townsfolk, the whole choir was soon ablaze and only the great central tower seems to have prevented the conflagration from destroying the whole church. When it had finally burnt itself out, the choir was a complete ruin, but the nave and western transepts as well as the crypt, the Chapels of St Anselm and St Andrew and the adjoining towers which bear the same names were still intact. Faithful to their Rule and the *Opus Dei*, which was the central occupation of their lives, the monastic community established itself in the nave and continued its normal liturgical life while plans were made for a rebuilding of the shattered choir. Within a month they installed Becket's successor, Richard of Dover, with as much ceremony as they could manage in what remained of the priory church.

Master William of Sens was selected as the architect, possibly because of the connections of the Church of Sens with Thomas Becket's exile, and it is his conception of the cathedral choir that we see today. Work began in

1175 and we have a remarkably detailed account from the monastic chronicler, Gervase, our authority both for the details of the fire and for the rebuilding between 1174 and 1184 when Archbishop Richard died.

While William of Sens was on a scaffolding in the crossing between the eastern transepts, probably superintending the placing of the vault in position, the scaffolding collapsed. He was flung to the ground fifty feet (fifteen metres) below, suffering such injuries that he was unable to continue the work even from a litter, and was compelled to resign his post and return to France where he died in August 1180. By that year a successor, William the Englishman, had been appointed. Work was sufficiently far advanced by Easter Even for the monks, with Archbishop Richard at their head, to come in solemn procession to their new choir for the great Easter Mass.

The work proceeded at an impressive speed. Within four years, by 1184 when the chronicle of Gervase comes to an end, the choir and presbytery were virtually completed and the work on the eastern crypt well in hand. This was designed as a pilgrimage or shrine chapel for the better accommodation of the body of St Thomas and for the pilgrims who were coming to Canterbury to venerate the sacred relics of the martyr. Even at this stage, the monks were probably planning to use this only as a temporary resting place until a much grander chapel could be built above. It is this eastern crypt in the Gothic style which one enters from the Romanesque gloom of the western undercroft of Our Lady.

When the work on the eastern crypt was well in hand the masons of William the Englishman were able to construct the great flight of steps to the platform on which the High Altar stands. Then they continued the steps to the pavement of the Trinity Chapel which formed the upper storey of the eastern crypt, rising twenty-five feet above the level of the ground outside. This was planned deliberately as a grand climax to the liturgical pattern of the whole building, with the Marble Chair of the Primates at the head of the steps and the chapel beyond. Here the relics of the 'holy blissful martyr' were destined to be enshrined when the building with its windows and eastern extension, the Corona, were completed.

During the primacy of Archbishop Baldwin, an austere Cistercian monk who was enthroned in 1185, the priory was engaged in opposing a scheme which he had produced for setting up a rival establishment of Canons Regular at Hackington just outside the city of Canterbury. It was suspected that this was intended to supplant the Benedictines of Christ Church and remove from them their traditional privilege of electing successive archbishops. Though Baldwin was foiled by their opposition to his scheme, his successor,

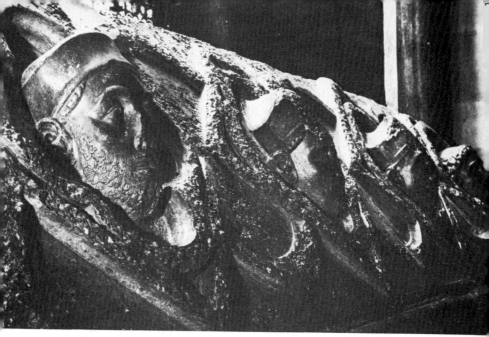

*Early-thirteenth-century heads on the tomb of Archbishop Hubert Walter.*

Hubert Walter, continued to pursue the idea of an electoral college. To get away from Canterbury, he purchased the Manor of Lambeth near the royal Palace of Westminster, proposing to establish his collegiate foundation there. But even his power and influence were not as great at Rome as those of the monks of the cathedral priory, and the Pope quashed the whole scheme in 1198. The only result of it all was that the Archbishop and his successors down to the present day have used their house or palace at Lambeth as their London residence.

In his last years Hubert Walter seems to have established happy relations with the monks. He has the distinction of having been buried, in 1205, in the newly completed Trinity Chapel in what is now the oldest surviving tomb in the cathedral. The monks soon had cause to mourn the demise of their archbishop. After some preliminary attempts to elect one of their own number as his successor, the monks accepted King John's nominee, one John de Gray, Bishop of Norwich, who was duly enthroned. A deputation was then sent to Rome at the expense of the King to secure the approval of the Pope. But the masterful Innocent III was determined to have as archbishop his friend Stephen Langton, an English cardinal living in Rome and attached to the Papal Curia. The election of John de Gray was set aside. In vindictive spite King John exiled all the monks to France where they found refuge at the Abbey of St Omer while the services in the cathedral were maintained by their rivals at St Augustine's Abbey. They remained in exile from 1207 until 1213, when the Interdict which Innocent eventually imposed upon England began to have its effect. John finally submitted, accepted Langton, and allowed the monks to return.

Stephen Langton must be numbered among the greatest archbishops at Canterbury. He is best remembered in the history of the cathedral for his devotion to the memory of St Thomas. The expression of this reached its climax on 7 July 1220 at a ceremony of the greatest magnificence, when he presided over the translation of the martyr's remains from the eastern crypt to the completed shrine in the Trinity Chapel. Its splendour was to dazzle the Christian Church in Northern Europe for the next three centuries. This shrine was to draw pilgrims up the great flights of steps to kneel around the chapel in prayer and worship at the round of masses and services which were maintained independently of the normal liturgical life of the choir below until the Reformation.

A contemporary panel of glass in one of the Miracle Windows of the Trinity Chapel gives us some idea of what this famous shrine looked like at the time of its completion in 1220. It stood in the middle of the chapel pavement on a stone base. The body was enclosed in an iron chest which was placed inside a wooden coffin covered with plates of gold and set with precious stones and jewels. Many of these were gifts from great kings and wealthy nobles, like the celebrated ruby known as the Regale of France, presented by Louis VII when he came on pilgrimage in 1179. Over the shrine was suspended a canopy which hung from the vault above. It appears to have been made of wood painted with sacred pictures and this was raised from time to time by one of the monks who were the guardians of the shrine.

In addition to the shrine itself, pilgrims were accustomed to make a round of visits to spots associated with St Thomas. These included the Corona where a part of his skull was exposed in a silver reliquary; the empty tomb in the eastern crypt; and the place of martyrdom in the north-west transept where the 'altare ad punctum ensis' stood, the sword point which finally slew the martyr being preserved there in a special case for the veneration of the pilgrims. A statue of the martyr, with lights burning before it, was placed before the altar and among other objects for awed pilgrims to venerate was a piece of the martyr's brain under rock crystal and his gold ring. For three centuries the Jubilee of the martyrdom and the translation was celebrated with much splendour until 1470 when great crowds came to rejoice at the victory and accession of the Yorkist King Edward IV and the fall of the House of Lancaster.

When the translation ceremonies were over, the treasury of the Archbishop was exhausted and for years to come his successors were in debt. No major work to the fabric took place for a century and a half. During the priorate of Henry of Eastry from 1285 to 1331 the parclose stone screen which runs all around the choir was built. This must have given the monks welcome privacy for their offices as the pilgrims streamed continuously up to the shrine area, as well as reducing the draughts inevitable in a building this size with its many doors and windows.

Eastry managed to put the finances of the priory on a sound footing and to clear it of the debts which he inherited when he came to his office. He rebuilt the Chapter House and constructed the great seat for the prior and the stalls for the monks around the walls. The building which was once the monks' brewery in the Green Court, as well as the Almonry Chapel which disappeared in 1859, and the Chequer building destroyed in 1886 all belong to the same period.

The last of the primates to be canonized was St Edmund Rich of Abingdon who was enthroned in 1234 and died in exile in 1240 at the Abbey of Pontigny where his shrine still stands behind the High Altar in the Abbey Church. He does not seem to have made much impact on the life of the monastery or the cathedral, but seems to have spent much of his time in conflict with the king. The exalted nature of the office of archbishop both in Church and State led to frequent conflicts such as these between the Plantagenets seeking to extract more money from their subjects in general and the Church in particular, and the archbishops protesting against the tyranny of the secular power. The fourteenth century saw the gradual decline of the Church spiritually, a decline hastened by the Black Death which destroyed, roughly, one in every three members of the population including at least two archbishops. Only four of the monks of Christ Church Priory died because the conditions under which the community lived were much superior to those of the world outside the Precincts.

John Stratford, who came to Canterbury from the great See of Winchester in 1333, was a statesman and administrator and one of the first of the great princes of the Church whose involvement with politics and with the interests of the Papacy, which not infrequently rewarded them for their services with the coveted cardinal's 'red hat', allowed them to live in great state and to be buried in one of those handsome tombs which are such a feature of the interior of the cathedral.

The last quarter of this century saw the death and burial of Edward the Black Prince at Michaelmas 1376 as well as the dreadful murder of his contemporary Archbishop Simon of Sudbury during the Peasants' Revolt in 1381. The Black Prince seems to have had a special love for the priory where he may have been educated by the monks. His noble tomb in the Trinity Chapel, the lovely chantry in the crypt now used by the Huguenot congregation, and his generous benefactions to the cathedral at his death in 1376 are eloquent witness to this affection. Perhaps the quiet ordered life of the monastery and its daily round of worship and prayer attracted him by its sharp contrast to the life of the court and the camp to which he was born. The creation of a Perpendicular chantry out of two Romanesque chapels in the crypt, where priests were to pray for the souls of the Prince and his wife, the beautiful Joan of Kent, mark the beginning of the great campaign which was to leave the cathedral with its imposing nave and Perpendicular towers. This work was begun in 1363 and followed by the erection of beautiful screens around the altar of the neighbouring chapel of Our Lady Undercroft where the Prince really wished to be buried.

A decade or so later the Norman nave was demolished and replaced by the present glorious structure under the direction of the great royal architect Henry Yevele. The south wall of the Romanesque cloister which leaned against the nave was also demolished as a necessary consequence of this. The community decided to rebuild the Great Cloister, beginning with the missing south alley and so rebuild the Chapter House at the same time. The Romanesque western facade of the Church with its two towers remained temporarily in position. The new nave was built from east to west, the work being completed with the great west window in the early years of the fifteenth century.

The moving spirit behind this great campaign of rebuilding was the treasurer of the monastery, Dom Thomas Chillenden. After the murder of Simon of Sudbury, work seems to have proceeded slowly. As England settled down again under Richard II and Sudbury's successor, William Courtenay, funds became more plentiful. When Chillenden succeeded the saintly Prior Finch in 1391 work went ahead with speed. At the time of his death in 1411 the nave was completed, the magnificent pulpitum screen was erected at the entrance to the choir, with another screen, built in the time of Prior Eastry, forming the east side. At the same time a grand new altar piece was erected in the choir. Great improvements were also made on the north side of the Precincts to the house now known as Chillenden Chambers and the pentise which leads from there to the Norman gate of the Green Court was built, as well as an upper storey added to the gate itself. Work on the cloister began when Archbishop Courtenay died in 1396 leaving a considerable legacy for the rebuilding of the demolished south alley and his coat of arms appears several times in the cloister, along with that of his successor, Thomas Arundel. Since the coat of arms of Archbishop Chichele, who was enthroned in 1414, appears in one bay it is presumed that the work on the rebuilding of the cloister was finished about that year, just after Chillenden had died and been succeeded by John Wodnesburgh. It is clear that the monastic community had run out of money after they had exhausted Courtenay's gift of £200. The profusion of coats of arms, some 810 in all, which adorn the vaulting of the west, north and east alleys appear to commemorate the benefactions of many notable folk which enabled the rebuilding to be completed.

The reign of Henry IV saw much of this work in process. His death in 1413 and his subsequent burial near the shrine in the Trinity Chapel was an important event in the cathedral's history. Chichele was primate all through the reign of his son, the warrior Henry V, and played some part in government while the king was abroad. He was at Canterbury to welcome him back after the famous victory at Agincourt. In his time the transformation of the west front took place with the erection of a new Perpendicular Gothic tower on the south-west side, the old tower of Lanfranc's time being left to present an

*The covered passageway known as the pentise.*

*The Pilgrim Steps.*

assymetrical facade for another four hundred years. During the rebuilding of this bell tower, in which the modern ring is hung, the south-west transept was also rebuilt in the fashionable late Gothic style. Then the Romanesque chapel of St Michael, with its upper storey of All Saints was demolished and the present rich and elaborate chapels erected instead. This was done at the expense of the aristocratic Duchess Margaret, one of the Holland family, who had married first Edmund Beaufort, a son of John of Gaunt, and then the Plantagenet Prince Thomas, Duke of Clarence, a brother of Henry V. The tomb of the Duchess and her two husbands, with their effigies placed in the centre of the chapel are among the most impressive monuments in the cathedral.

At this stage in its history the cathedral priory was at the height of its fame as a great centre of devotion and culture. Many indeed were the illustrious visitors who came as pilgrims to the famous shrine. These included the emperors of both east and west. In 1400 the

OPPOSITE: *The vault of the south-west porch.*

Emperor Manuel came from Constantinople seeking help against the Ottoman Turks who were to destroy his empire just half a century later, while the Holy Roman Emperor Sigismund was here in 1416. The arms of both empires appear on the cloister vault.

The accession of the little King Henry VI, a most pious sovereign, saw a long succession of royal pilgrimages to the shrine while the usurper, Edward IV, was an even more regular pilgrim and supporter of the monks. The north-west transept was rebuilt at this time as the heraldry of the vault indicates. In the process the setting of the martyrdom of St Thomas, which had survived intact for three hundred years, was transformed so that it is hard to recapture the feeling of that event today. This is partly because of the insertion of the huge royal window in the north wall. The glass in it was the gift of Edward IV and he, his wife and the royal children all appear in the middle of the window. It commemorated the fact that his ancestor Edward I had been married inside the cloister door to Margaret of France in 1299. Only a few years after the window was completed Edward IV died prematurely and the Yorkist line ended in tragedy with the mysterious disappearance of the two princes whose portraits appear in the glass. This was followed by the death in battle on Bosworth Field of their uncle, the usurping Richard III in 1485.

With the accession of Henry VII and the establishment of the Tudor dynasty, his chief minister and adviser John Morton became archbishop. This powerful and wealthy man who subsequently became a cardinal appears to have persuaded Prior Sellinge and his monks, without much difficulty, to put in hand the building of the great central tower which had been contemplated for a long time since the demolition of the Romanesque 'Angel Steeple'. This last great addition to the cathedral exterior with its elaborate interior fan vaulting was no doubt largely paid for by Morton himself, at a probable cost in modern money of at least a million pounds. The tower was finally completed under the scholarly and gentle William Warham, who became archbishop in 1503.

Work began on rebuilding the great gatehouse of the Precincts on the south side in 1507. The heraldry on its facade suggests that it may have been intended as a memorial to the little Prince Arthur, eldest son of Henry VII, who died shortly after his marriage to Katherine of Aragon. This Christ Church Gate is one of the most handsome entrances to any cathedral precinct and marks the end of a long campaign of building which had begun with the erection of Yevele's nave more than a century before. The monks may have intended to round off the Corona with a steeple, but were not allowed the time to do this or anything else.

A great royal visit took place at Whitsun 1520, when Henry VIII, who had come to the throne in 1509, came as a pilgrim together with Queen Katherine and her mighty nephew the Emperor Charles V. The presence of his all-powerful minister Cardinal Wolsey on this occasion may account for his coat of arms on the vault of the recently finished Christ Church Gate.

Within ten years Wolsey had fallen, Henry was seeking a divorce from Katherine, Luther's doctrines were spreading all over Europe and the era of pilgrimages and monasteries in England was rapidly coming to an end. When Thomas Cromwell succeeded Wolsey as Henry's chief minister in 1529 he continued the work of dissolving the religious houses (which Wolsey had begun) with awful ruthlessness. By 1538 it was clear that all were to be swept away. In that year Henry's commissioners descended on Canterbury and demolished the shrine, sending the vast spoils of gold and jewels to London for the benefit of the King. Instructions were given that the bones were to be burnt and the ashes scattered, so it must be presumed that this was done, though romantic ideas occasionally circulate about the body being secretly hidden by the monks before the commissioners arrived.

When St Augustine's Abbey was disssolved, the Christ Church monks must have known that their community would soon share the same fate. In fact it was one of the last to be dissolved, the commissioners arriving on 4 April 1540 and accepting the surrender in the Chapter House. In contrast to the judicial murders of the abbots at Glastonbury and Colchester, and the butchery of the monks of the London Charterhouse, there was no violence or bloodshed at Canterbury. The community was presumably too cowed by this time to offer any resistance. The prior, Dom Thomas Goldwell, and most of the monks accepted good pensions and disappeared into obscure retirement, but some twenty-seven monks accepted posts on the foundation, six of the seniors becoming prebendaries (canons residentiary in modern parlance), twelve others becoming minor canons and the youngest filling humbler posts.

In April 1541 the new statutes prepared by Cranmer and Henry VIII were published, setting up a foundation like those of the older cathedrals of St Paul's, Salisbury and Wells, with a dean at the head and twelve prebendaries or canons as well as minor canons to maintain the daily offices and mass. Like other cathedrals with a monastic past, Canterbury had a little group of twelve poor folk to carry out various tasks around the church. These were known as bedesmen and are still conspicuous in the life of the cathedral on Sundays and high feasts, in their gowns with a Tudor rose on the back, leading the processions with white staves in their hands.

In addition, an entirely original college of priests known as the Six Preachers was brought into existence to present to the church people of the Diocese of Canterbury both the traditional doctrines of the Church and also the new ideas which were emerging from the writings of Luther and other reformers of Continental Europe. Strangely, although no other cathedral seems to have thought it worthwhile to add a similar group of priests to its foundation, the Six Preachers of Canterbury Cathedral have survived as an institution to this day. They were certainly kept busy during the century of controversy between the last years of Henry VIII's reign and the restoration of Charles II in 1660. Perhaps wisely, the new dean, Dr Nicholas Wotton, who succeeded the last prior Thomas Goldwell, was seldom in his cathedral city, and so managed to avoid ecclesiastical controversy. A most able diplomat and greatly trusted by Henry VIII, who left him a considerable sum of money in his will, he was usually abroad in the service of his country, which may have been why he kept his head on his shoulders and died in his bed when so many other leading ecclesiastics finished up miserably at the stake or on the scaffold.

Without a strong presence in their midst to pilot the new order with its English Prayer Book and radical changes in liturgy and theology, the canons fell into either non-residence or endless quarrels and intrigues. Archbishop Cranmer's well-intentioned exertions on behalf of a reformed and purified church were often frustrated and finally brought to a tragic end by zealots of all persuasions. The treasures of plate, vestments, and ornaments of all kinds, with which great artists and craftsmen had glorified the magnificent cathedral in monastic days, were quickly dissipated and squandered by their unworthy successors. When the second dean, Mr Godwyn, succeeded Dean Wotton in 1567, very little remained.

The reign of Edward VI saw the passing of the Chantries Act which dissolved all the chantry foundations including those of the Black Prince and Henry IV, as well as that of Archbishop Warham. During Mary's reign from 1553 to 1558 an attempt was made to restore the ceremonies and liturgy of the Latin Rite, and after the burning of Cranmer the last of the cardinal archbishops, Reginald Pole, was appointed in his stead in 1556. He is best remembered for his gifts to the Chapter of the Almonry Buildings around the Mint Yard which links the Green Court with the city area of Northgate, and his memory is cherished by the King's School which moved into the buildings there in 1573 and has been there ever since.

Queen Elizabeth continued the custom of royal visits to

Canterbury though there was no longer any shrine there and pilgrimages had gone out of fashion. Her visit in 1573 was intended to honour Matthew Parker, who became archbishop at the beginning of her long reign. It certainly cost him a great deal of money as she came with a large train of courtiers who stayed at the former Abbey of St Augustine's, which had been turned into a royal palace after the Dissolution. As well as attending divine service in the cathedral she was entertained at a splendid banquet in the Archbishop's Palace at which she seems to have presided, sitting in state in the Marble Chair which was brought out of the cathedral for the occasion.

The religious wars which raged in Northern Europe at this time brought about a great influx of Huguenot refugees from Northern France and French-speaking Flanders into East Kent. On the orders of the Queen they were largely settled in Canterbury, being given the use of the crypt for assembly and worship, since that part of the cathedral had been neglected since the departure of the monks. Its eastern part was utilized as a coal cellar by the prebendaries who were beginning to settle down comfortably in large houses in the Precincts where they started to marry and raise families.

The reign of James I saw the rise of William Laud who was to become archbishop in the next reign and whose inept attempts to stamp out Puritanism and revive the life of the Church of England roused immense resentment in the powerful Puritan party which was to have a terrible effect on the life of the cathedral during the Great Rebellion. The reign of Charles I began with a royal visit, long remembered because of the first appearance at Canterbury of his young French bride, Henrietta Maria, who Charles had met at Dover.

Laud was effectively in charge of affairs in the Church of England for several years before becoming primate in 1633, since the official Archbishop, George Abbot, was suspended owing to a sad accident in which he shot one of his keepers while hunting. The Laudian regime saw the cathedral enriched with a new and well-furnished altar as well as the font which still stands in the nave. In 1634 the Archbishop held a visitation of his cathedral in which he stated that it was his intention 'to provide diligently that the praises of God be celebrated constantly morning and evening in the Cathedral', an ideal which has been preserved tenaciously for more than three centuries to the present day.

For all his care for worship, and the maintenance of the fabric as well as the common life of the foundation, Laud's methods of dealing with the situation at Canterbury and throughout his province was a prelude to disaster. From the end of 1639 to 1642 constant disturbances in the religious life of the city were an ominous prelude to the storm which burst on the cathedral at the end of August 1642. A troop of soldiers took possession of the building and virtually sacked the choir, overthrowing the Communion Table, smashing furniture, tearing down the tapestry and using the great statue of Christ over the south gate as target practice. During a brief respite after this before war actually broke out, the King and Queen attended Divine Service in Canterbury at Christmas although soon the daily services were discontinued.

At the end of 1643 an Act of Parliament abolished deans and chapters. There was now no body empowered to deal with the iconoclasts who set to work to destroy the famous stained glass windows and the medieval statues which appear to have survived the Reformation intact. Headed by a renegade priest, Richard Culmer, known as 'Blue Dick' because he refused to wear a black cassock like the loyal Anglican clergy, they stormed into the cathedral with the Parliamentary Commissioners. Despite the presence of some of the faithful, Culmer and his satellites directed their attention to everything they deemed 'popish', especially Edward IV's window in the Martyrdom Transept, where Culmer, armed with a ladder and a pike, 'rattled down Becket's glassy bones'. For his services to the Puritan cause he was made a Six Preacher along with others of the same outlook. For some seventeen miserable years, the affairs of the great Church of Christ were administered by such men as this: fanatics who allowed the fabric to fall into disrepair, seizing good houses in the Precincts as their lodgings, plundering the fittings and cutting down the oaks and other trees for the money they fetched, while the cathedral resounded with their extemporary prayers and interminable sermons. Loyal Anglicans like William Somner, the famous antiquary who rescued the cathedral font from demolition, must have despaired of any recovery of the Church of England. Then, within two years of the Protector's death, the Monarchy, and with it the Church, was restored amid scenes of delirious excitement and joy as Charles II returned.

He landed at Dover on Saturday, 25 May 1660 and stayed at St Augustine's, attending Divine Service in the cathedral the next day. 'The people seemed glad to hear the Common Prayer again', according to Clarendon and one can only suppose that the loyal clergy returned to their duties again for the occasion. The Puritan ministers were sent packing and very soon William Juxon was installed at Lambeth Palace in time to crown Charles II. Thomas Turner was, at last, able to claim the deanery to which he had been appointed seventeen years before. Twelve new loyal canons were installed,

The seventeenth-century doors of the
Christ Church Gate.

The canopy of Archbishop Tenison's
throne in the nave.

together with minor canons, six preachers and lay clerks and other
servants of the church who had suffered grievously in these hard
times. The Chapter promptly set about recovering its lost revenues
from leases. By the end of 1660 repairs to the fabric, the purchase of
altar plate, vergers' maces, a new lectern for the choir and other
furniture were all in hand at a cost of £8000, a vast sum of money for
those times.

With the Restoration the cathedral settled down to a settled life of
worship under worthy but rather dull deans, prebendaries and non-
resident archbishops. The Palace at Canterbury had been wrecked
during the Commonwealth period so thoroughly that the primates
only attempted to rebuild it at the end of the nineteenth century. The
very end of the eighteenth century saw the cathedral choir well
wainscoted to keep out draughts, and morning and evening prayer
sung daily but, from 1790, Holy Communion celebrated only once a
month instead of once a week. During the primacy of William
Howley there began to be a stirring of new life. The Ecclesiastical
Commission started to prune the capitular bodies, reducing the
canons of Canterbury from twelve to six. The Gothic Revival and the
Oxford Movement were soon in full swing and for a century and a
half there has been much activity on every front.

The fine Corinthian throne given by Archbishop Tenison was
replaced in 1844 by the 'Gothick' throne, still in the choir, a gift from

Howley himself. The venerable Romanesque tower of Lanfranc's Church was demolished in 1834 and replaced by the existing north-west tower which is a careful copy of its neighbour making a symmetrical west front of early fifteenth-century uniformity in style.

The reign of Dean Alford saw the erection of the stone staircase, known as the Deans' Stairs on the north side of the cathedral, and the building of a large, new cathedral library alongside the Chapter House, using part of the remains of Lanfranc's eleventh century dormitory. A number of monastic buildings including the old Chequer House were demolished, probably to save the expense of maintenance at a time of financial stringency, since the management of the extensive estates of cathedral chapters was taken over by the Ecclesiastical Commissioners and the income used for the general betterment of the life of the Church all over England. Alford did much to reinvigorate the worship of the cathedral, a welcome lead which was followed by his successor, the learned Dr Payne-Smith. It was early in his time, in 1872, that a fire broke out in the roof of the Trinity Chapel as a result of carelessness on the part of a plumber who put his pipe, still alight, in his jacket pocket and left it on the chapel roof where it set fire to the rafters. (This only came to light some sixty years later when a written confession from the culprit was found after his death.) Thanks to the stone vaulting of William the Englishman and prompt action by the Canterbury Volunteer Fire Brigade the fire was soon under control. In due course the roof was repaired and assumed its present appearance. Another fire broke out in 1876 in the south-west tower during the cleaning of the clock. This, too, was extinguished rapidly although two lives were lost in the blaze.

The latter part of the nineteenth century saw the recovery of the crypt for use by the cathedral authorities. The eastern crypt was cleansed of its coal and other accumulated rubbish, and provided with a new floor while the Huguenot congregation was persuaded to move from the south aisle of the western crypt into the much more suitable and compact area of the Black Prince's Chantry, where they continue to worship to this day. Among various works of restoration begun during the last years of Queen Victoria's reign was the repair of St Anselm's Chapel which brought to light the painting of St Paul and the viper in 1882. They also renovated the great Chapter House of the monks in 1897.

The great expectations of a golden age at the start of the twentieth century were soon shattered by the First World War. Some stone work was renewed on Bell Harry Tower and other parts of the fabric, but it was not until the appointment of Dr G.K.A. Bell as dean in 1924

*The Black Prince's Chantry, now the Huguenot church in the crypt.*

that the cathedral really moved into the bustling life of the new century. The formation of the Friends of the Cathedral, the inauguration of the summer festivals, and the broadcasting of choral services led to the development of the musical foundation with the opening of a resident choir school in an old house in the Brick Walk of the Precincts. The restoration of tombs and wall paintings began with the support of money from the Friends. Among work undertaken before 1939 was the restoration of the Norman Water Tower and the painting of the shields on the cloister vault in their heraldic colours.

All the ancient glass was removed on the outbreak of war and stored away for safety, while the famous tombs and monuments were protected by sandbags, corrugated iron and concrete shelters. When the awful 'Baedeker raid' took place in reprisal for allied raids on Cologne on the night of 1 June 1942, a well-trained company of fire guards was ready and prepared on the roofs of the great building. As fire bombs rained down on the church they were promptly dealt with by the cathedral watchers, so that unlike Coventry Cathedral, the cathedral was saved, though much of the old city was destroyed. The cathedral library, constructed in the nineteenth century, was almost completely wrecked by a high explosive bomb and many of the houses in the Precincts were severely damaged. Some of the King's School buildings, including the Dining Hall in the Green Court, were shattered. After V.E. Day in May 1945 the work of restoration began in earnest. Soon ancient glass was being replaced in windows, and tombs and monuments released from their protective coverings. On 11 July 1946 King George VI and Queen Elizabeth, accompanied by the young Princess Elizabeth, visited Canterbury to attend a great service of thanksgiving for the preservation of the cathedral from destruction. In 1954 a new library, designed by John Denman replaced the bombed one, and in 1966 an additional library building was opened on the east side of the Water Tower garden.

At the end of 1974 the newly appointed archbishop, Dr Donald Coggan, launched an appeal for funds to restore the crumbling stonework and the decaying stained glass. The money was also to provide new bells, a renovated organ and to increase the endowment for the musical foundation, as well as for the restoration of the mural paintings. This work is still in hand, something like four million pounds having been raised by public subscription in the last ten years.

The most historic occasion of modern times occurred on 29 May 1982 when, in bright sunshine, Archbishop Robert Runcie and the cathedral Chapter received the Pope John Paul II, attended by five cardinals, and Charles, Prince of Wales, at the doors of the cathedral. They then proceeded to join with a most distinguished ecumenical congregation and millions of viewers on television in a unique celebration of praise and worship. The lovely music and beautiful language combined with a wonderful atmosphere of Christian fellowship and architectural splendour to make the most memorable and joyous day in the long history of 'Christ's Glorious Church'.

*Chapter Two*

# A WALK AROUND THE CATHEDRAL EXTERIOR AND PRECINCTS

T HE BEST APPROACH to the cathedral is by way of the West Gate of the city and the main street. Passing such attractive landmarks as the Weavers and the almshouse known as Eastbridge Hospital in the medieval area of the city, one reaches Mercery Lane on the left hand side of the street. At the far end of this famous, though much modernized, thoroughfare, the west towers of the cathedral can be seen rising above the Tudor gatehouse which is known as the Christ Church Gate. This was constructed in place of an earlier gate as the main entrance to the south side of the Precincts a few years after the erection of the great central tower and only a quarter of a century before the fall of the monastery in 1540. In front of the gate is a small open space where the old Buttermarket of the city was held, which today affords a beautiful view of the gate and the cathedral beyond.

### The Christ Church Gate

A wide Tudor arch for carriages and a smaller postern gate for pedestrians lead to the Cathedral Precincts and these retain the fine wooden doors which were made in 1660 to replace the original doors destroyed by the Parliamentarian soldiers in 1643. They are carved with the arms of Archbishop Juxon and Dean Turner with much other decoration characteristic of the late seventeenth century. Over the gateway are two chambers which in 1541 were assigned to one of the Six Preachers as an official dwelling, but are now used for office and storage purposes.

The lower part of the gate is built of stone and the chambers above are built of brick faced with stone. The windows which light these

*Angels with Passion emblems on the Christ Church Gate.*

two rooms are grouped on each side of a tall canopied niche which once contained a statue of Christ until Puritan troops used it for target practice in August 1642. It was completely destroyed in mid-December 1643, when, egged on by the fanatical Puritan Preacher, Richard Culmer, another group of soldiers lassoed the statue and pulled it down.

It is not certain who was the designer of the gate. The use of brick and stone suggests John Wastell who is known to have been the master mason responsible for the great central 'Bell Harry' tower which looms up a few yards away and where the same materials are employed, but the style suggests that it may have been another distinguished master mason flourishing in the early Tudor period, Robert Vertue, who was in charge of work on a new tower at St Augustine's Abbey nearby at the same time that Wastell was building one at the cathedral.

The great feature of the Christ Church Gate which catches the eye is the brilliant series of coats of arms which tell us a lot about the period when the gate was being built and some of those connected with this work. The upper range of these on the south side of the gate are a modern restoration showing the instruments of Christ's Passion: twelve shields borne by angels, ranged on either side of the empty niche. The lower range of shields form a frieze just over the gate itself. These are carved and painted and lend some colour to an inscription below which has been re-cut stating in Latin that the gate was constructed in 1507.

An examination of the shields lends weight to the theory advanced recently by the antiquary, Philip Blake, that the gate was intended as a memorial to Arthur, Prince of Wales. He was the eldest son of Henry VII and his destined heir who died at the age of sixteen in 1502 having married the Spanish Princess Katherine of Aragon in 1499. The imposing Royal Arms in the centre of the frieze is that of Henry VII and is flanked on each side by the Portcullis and Tudor Rose which were badges of the royal house. The arms both of Prince Arthur (surmounted by a princely coronet) and of Princess Katherine appear also with those of several noblemen: Sir Henry Guldeford, Sir William Scott, Sir John Fyneaux, Sir Edward Poynings, Sir Thomas Howard (Duke of Norfolk), Sir George Neville and Sir Charles Somerset (Earl of Worcester). Nearly all these knights were favourites of Henry VII and had close connections with Prince Arthur and his wife, while several of them held estates in Kent. It is therefore possible to entertain the suggestion that the gate was indeed intended as a memorial to the short-lived Prince and that some of the cost at least may have been met by these wealthy noblemen as a way of commemorating a young man 'born to be King'.

What seems to be certain is that the gate was not finished in 1507 and, perhaps, building work went on here for another decade. The arms of the penultimate prior, Thomas Goldstone II appear over the postern gate and also on the vaulting inside the gate, together with the arms of Cardinal Wolsey, who became Archbishop of York in 1514. These appear on the vault with those of his contemporary Archbishop Warham of Canterbury and those of the last prior, Thomas Goldwell (a gold well on a sable ground), who only took office in 1517 on the death of Thomas Goldstone. The vault has a fine Tudor rose as a boss in its centre with other heraldic bosses, including the arms attributed by medieval heralds to Thomas Becket. By contrast with the south front, that on the north side has only the arms of Henry VIII and those of the priory with a Tudor rose and a Portcullis. Interestingly the presence of Renaissance motifs – pilasters and supporting capitals – suggests an Italian influence such as appears elsewhere in England in early sixteenth-century work.

In its present form the appearance of the Christ Church Gate owes much to a great restoration begun in 1931 and completed in 1935 under the direction of the distinguished architect W.D. Caroe, then surveyor to the cathedral. The two twin turrets which are now a prominent feature of the design were demolished in about 1803 and replaced by careful replicas in 1937, so that the gate with its repainted heraldry now looks much as it did some four hundred and seventy years ago. The work of restoration was undertaken by the Friends of the Cathedral with generous support from Dame Janet Stancomb-Wills and her sister Mrs. Yda Richardson. Both these ladies are commemorated by lozenges bearing their coats of arms on the front of the gate.

Just inside the gate, on the left side, is the small cottage occupied until recently by the gate porter whose duties included the opening of the gates early in the morning and their closure after the ringing of curfew at 9 pm. The cathedral shop and a row of dwelling houses extends on this side of the Precincts, mostly from the early nineteenth century, with frontages composed of the mathematical tiles fashionable at that time. Modern office blocks, housing mostly firms of lawyers, continue the line of buildings down to the gates of the Old Palace, which are adorned with the arms of Archbishop Frederick Temple (1897 to 1903). From the fall of Laud and the temporary abolition of the archbishopric, the palace had fallen into a state of dilapidation and become a series of tenements let out to local citizens. The archbishops made no attempt to rebuild the palace after 1660 but established themselves comfortably at Lambeth. As a country residence they firstly used their handsome palace at Croydon and then, after the sale of Croydon Palace in the nineteenth century, a pleasant house in large grounds at Addington near Croydon, within the Diocese of Canterbury. The last primate to live there was Dr Benson. In the time of his successor, Dr Temple, the decision was made to sell Addington and with the proceeds to rebuild, on a relatively modest scale, the 'Old Palace' at Canterbury so that the archbishops could have a suitable residence close by their cathedral church. W.D. Caroe, the cathedral surveyor, was the architect. Between 1897 and 1899 a pleasant country house, complete with chapel and reception rooms as well as bedrooms for ordination candidates was constructed, incorporating in its design some medieval and Tudor remains of the original grandiose palace whose origins went back to the Domesday Book and which had played a considerable part in the dramatic events leading to the martyrdom of Thomas Becket on 29 December 1170.

## The South of the Nave

Facing the south side of the nave is a large rambling house which

*The south-west porch and bays of the nave.*

has now become the administrative centre of the cathedral Chapter
with a small hostel on the top floor. The origins of the house go back
to 1600 when one of the canons, Dr Richard Wood, built himself a
new house there which was rented later by another canon,
Archdeacon Kingsley, who enlarged it. Subsequent tenants, not
always members of the Chapter, continued to add to it from time to
time, and the last major additions, the porch with its four Doric
columns and the bay window above date from the very end of the
eighteenth century.

Looking at the cathedral from this porch one observes the rich
variety of architectural styles which have come to compose the whole
church over the centuries. At first sight, it appears that the great
central tower unites two separate late twelfth century and early
fifteenth-century parts: the eastern arm in French Gothic style, and
the western arm in the Perpendicular Gothic style. It soon becomes
apparent as one walks eastward around the outside that a large amount
of Romanesque work from the twelfth-century cathedral still
survives. This is most notable in the great western crypt, as well as

much of the lower walls of the eastern transepts and the towers which spring out of them, and the two small chapels of St Andrew and St Anselm, while in the south wall of the latter chapel is a magnificent window in Decorated style inserted by Prior Oxenden in 1336.

The nave consists of eight bays with an additional bay to engage the west towers. It occupies the same area as Lanfranc's Romanesque nave which was demolished to make way for the present one in 1378. Medieval churchmen did not think in terms of conservation so that after a century and a half of peace from architects and builders a new generation of monks would have accepted without demur the project of a grandiose new nave designed by one of the great architects of the Middle Ages, Henry Yevele, with the promise of much financial help from the Archbishop Simon of Sudbury. His coat of arms, the little white dog on a sable ground, appears in cloister, Chapter House and nave vaulting suggesting great interest in the building campaign which was now begun and was in fact to continue until the very end of the monastic regime a century and a half later. The brutal execution of Sudbury in 1381 does not seem to have hindered the work unduly, largely because of the energy and financial ability of the treasurer of the monastery, Dom Thomas Chillenden, who was elected prior in 1391 and remained in office until his death in 1411. Under his leadership the work advanced rapidly, the west window being in place by the end of the fourteenth century, though the glazing of the main lights had to wait for some decades, presumably owing to lack of funds.

### The South-West Porch

From this point outside the nave, the south-west tower and the porch below capture the eye. The south-west porch has been the way by which pilgrims and visitors have entered the cathedral since Saxon times when the 'suthdore' is referred to by the chronicler Eadmer. It is a commodious porch with a rich adornment of heraldry in its vault and many niches outside for statues. The statues themselves, as well as those which filled the empty niches along the south side of the nave, were all demolished by Puritan iconoclasts during 1642 and 1643. Soon after his installation as dean in 1857 the energetic Dr Henry Alford launched a scheme for replacing statues in the empty niches. He commissioned a Belgian sculptor, Theodore Pfyffers, to do the work, the money being contributed by public subscription and each statue costing £24. Representations of St Augustine of Canterbury, King Ethelbert, Queen Bertha and a number of archbishops and eminent personages connected with the cathedral soon appeared. In due course Queen Victoria, Albert the Prince Consort, Archbishop

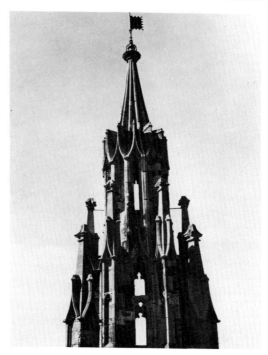

*A pinnacle of Bell Harry Tower.*

Sumner and the good Dean himself filled some of the vacant spaces 'in effigy'. The scheme was never completed and several niches are still empty, whilst many of the statues are wearing badly a century or more later, since Pfyffers was sadly a mediocre artist.

The porch is an imposing piece of work with a small chamber called the 'Parvis' Room above the heraldic vaulting which was constructed between 1414 and 1418. The shields on the vault suggest that it was intended to commemorate the great victory of the English army over the French at the Battle of Agincourt on 25 October 1415. This was followed by a great pontifical mass of thanksgiving in the cathedral celebrated by Archbishop Henry Chichele in the presence of King Henry V on his way home to London some weeks later. Since the arms of the King and the Archbishop both appear on the vaulting, along with sixteen coats of arms of noblemen who either fought with Henry at Agincourt or in the Hundred Years War, as well as others who were supporters of the House of Lancaster, the theory that this porch is a commemoration of Henry's famous victory is not lightly to be dismissed.

Perhaps the most unusual feature about the façade of the porch is a carving of an altar and reredos with a crucifix and figures of St Mary and St John over the main entrance. This is now generally supposed to be a represention of the celebrated '*altare ad punctum ensis*', the Altar of the Sword's Point which stood in the Martyrdom Transept so that the pilgrims of medieval England could venerate the broken sword point, which had administered the coup-de-grace to St Thomas, lying upon the altar in a special case.

It is supposed that alongside the representation of the altar would have been carved the murder of St Thomas with the four knights in the niches on either side. If the porch was completed by 1418 it may have been designed by Stephen Lote who was employed by the prior and convent in the first part of the fifteenth century taking over the work on the nave from Yevele after his death in 1400 and being responsible for the rebuilding of the Great Cloister.

The fine south-west bell tower which rises impressively above the porch was designed by Thomas de Mapilton. Work on it seems to have started in 1423, the year after the death of Henry V and continued to its completion ten years later. It has always been associated with Archbishop Chichele who contributed the large sum of £475 towards the work. It is an attractive tower, probably designed to match in height the old Norman tower on the north-west side which was pulled down in 1832. This was replaced by a copy of Mapilton's tower, creating the famous symmetrical façade with which we are familiar today; it serves as a perfect foil to the grandiose Bell Harry which, from a distance, can be seen rising between the two western towers.

In the gable between these towers is a very attractive and richly traceried window which lights the roof area over the centre of the nave. Beneath this is the great west window, dating from the beginning of the fifteenth century, with three tiers of seven lights and elaborate tracery. The west door is a ceremonial entrance for great occasions and stately processions but, since this end of the Precincts is built up close to the façade of the church, it is not an important part of the architectural composition as it would be in France, where one normally expects to find triple porches and much fine statuary. It has a shallow porch with a lierne vault and an iron grille only opened for processional occasions. Over the West Door is an insignificant figure of Christ the Good Shepherd in Pfyffers' most insipid style.

### The South-West Transept
Proceeding eastwards from the south-west porch we next reach the south-west transept. After the rebuilding of the nave under Yevele's

direction, the remodelling of the transepts to the west of the choir in a similar Perpendicular Gothic style followed naturally. We can suppose that the south-west transept with its huge window and heraldic vault was designed and carried out under the direction of the master masons who succeeded Yevele: namely Stephen Lote and Thomas Mapilton. The transept here has only one tall pinnacle on its western side. On the apex of the gable there is a small podium on which the figure of the angel from the summit of the pyramidal Norman tower was placed in *c.* 1430. The late Canon J.M.C. Crum suggested the interesting theory that the angel was not St Michael but Christ himself, the Angel of Mighty Counsel, from Isaiah IX v. 6 in the Vulgate version. The abominable Blue Dick Culmer in his Cathedral News from Canterbury tells, with relish, how one hundred men with a rope pulled down and destroyed this image 'with a great brazen crosse in his hand' in 1642.

The next stage in the remodelling of the western arm of the church can be seen in the Chapel of St Michael, and that of All Saints which forms the upper storey on the eastern side of the transept. From the amount of new white Lepine stone that can be seen both in the transept and these two chapels, it will be clear that a great deal of restoration of the stonework has been undertaken in the last few years. The old Romanesque chapels with their apses which stood on the east side of the transept were demolished just before 1437 when the Duchess Margaret (Holland) of Clarence commissioned and paid for the new work. By this time Thomas Mapilton had died and was replaced by Richard Beke. Appointed master of the works for life at the beginning of 1435 he remained in office until 1458, and designed the square-ended chapels.

From here can be seen a curious sight: the end of the simple stone tomb of Archbishop Stephen Langton, who died in 1228, sticking out through the wall of St Michael's Chapel into the churchyard. Just behind the flint wall which runs parallel to the cathedral at this point is the mound where the Romanesque bell tower dating back to the twelfth century stood. This campanile was seriously damaged by the great earthquake which was felt all over England on 21 May 1382. The destruction of the bells in this tower may have been the ultimate reason for the building of the south-west tower usually known as St Dunstan's in which the cathedral ring has been housed for so many centuries. (The campanile itself was repaired but was finally demolished at the time of the Dissolution.)

Now one can see Bell Harry towering over the whole of this great building. The monks may well have despaired of seeing their church completed with a worthy central tower at a time when so

*Bell Harry Tower.*

many cathedral and monastic churches were being crowned with splendid towers like those at York, Gloucester or Lincoln. On 4 August 1433, 'the first stone of the new work of the Angel Steeple was laid and blessed'. In the following years work went on in preparing for the lower stage of the tower internally, while the piers of the crossing were strengthened to bear the immense load which it was hoped would eventually be laid upon them. This was inevitably costly and after a century of rebuilding in the western part of the church even this wealthy foundation may have been under some financial stress. However in the last years of Prior Sellinge *c.* 1490 work began

*Detail of the exterior of St Anselm's Tower.*

above the line of the roof and we can see in this the energetic
patronage of Archbishop John Morton who chose John Wastell as the
master mason and approved the design for the tower as well as
supplying a great deal of the money needed for so grandiose a project
from his great personal wealth. The Reverend C.E. Woodruff
records that the convent spent over £4000 between Easter 1494 and
Michaelmas 1496, purchasing some '480,000 redde bryks' for the
inside part of the tower, the exterior being clothed with stone from
Caen and Merstham so that the tower harmonizes with the rest of the
building. It is on this outer skin of stone that Morton's Cardinal's hat
and badges are carved to commemorate his great share in the building
of this noble tower. On the fan vaulting inside the church are the coats
of arms of Henry VII, Prior Goldstone II, and those of Archbishops
Morton and Warham. We can thus date the finishing of the tower
with its four great pinnacles to about 1504.

*The exterior of the Corona.*

The small Norman tower which projects from the south-east transept acts as a happy foil to its mighty neighbour. Its pyramidal cap or spirelet and the beautiful carving on this tower reminds us of the amount of work of the Romanesque period which was preserved by William of Sens during his transformation of the burnt-out choir into a glorious French Gothic building between 1175 and 1178. Though the aisles and transepts in their present form are mainly his work, the older church can be discerned outside not only in the crypt, but also in the band of interlacing arches which runs from the western transepts right around the eastern ones and only terminates where the Romanesque chapels of St Anselm and St Andrew link up with William the Englishman's Trinity Chapel ambulatory. Perhaps we can attribute this lovely arcading to Blitherus, a Saxon master of the works described in 1090 as 'the very distinguished master of the craftsmen and director of the beautiful church'.

### The South-East Transept
Looking at the south-east transept from outside, the Transitional

OPPOSITE: *Prior Oxenden's fourteenth-century window.*

nature of the church is very apparent. The windows in the south façade are all round-headed as if they belonged to the earlier church but the large oculus or rose in the gable gives a very French Gothic air to the transept, and windows with pointed heads fill the clerestory area west and east providing a visual link with the clerestory of the choir. As one walks east the fine Decorated window of 1366 inserted by Prior Oxenden in the Chapel of St Anselm comes into view, looking in no way out of place in its distinctively Romanesque setting. Beyond this is the glorious outline of the Trinity Chapel, very Gothic and very French with its sweeping lead roof and flying buttresses, all culminating in the singular and bulky mass of the Corona.

## The Corona

The view from the platform on the unfinished top storey of the Corona embraces the lawns and gardens which were once two graveyards: that of the citizens to the west; and that of the monks to the east. Until 1841 a wall with a Romanesque gateway separated the two, but in that year the gate was moved and is now the entrance to the garden which was once the canons' bowling green, but has been the Kent County War Memorial since 1918. The area to the south has only modern houses now, since much of this area of the city was destroyed in the raid of 1942 and had to be rebuilt after the war. Popularly known as the 'Oaks', although these were wantonly cut down during the Commonwealth, this stretch of grass is now fringed by limes. A great oriental plane tree stands close to the War Memorial Garden, where magnolias, hibiscus and palms can all be found as well as many English shrubs and flowers. The garden wall of Number 15 as well as the north and south walls of the Memorial Garden are of lovely mellow brick; bee-boles can be seen, at intervals, along them.

The east wall of the Memorial Garden is, in fact, the medieval flint wall of the city. The bastion in the middle of this stretch of wall was converted into a delightful memorial chapel after the First World War at the same time that the fine cross was placed in the middle of the garden. Each year in August, during Canterbury Cricket Week a celebration of Holy Communion is held in the chapel and wreaths laid on the cross at a special ceremony in memory of those men and women who died in the two World Wars. Apart from the well-kept lawns and flowers in the garden visitors can hardly fail to notice the ancient mulberry tree in the north-west corner which tradition says was planted to commemorate the Restoration of Charles II in 1660. The great creeper, a wistaria, which runs along the west wall is similarly said to have been planted to commemorate the publication

*The ruins of the Romanesque infirmary.*

of the Authorised Version of the Bible in the reign of James I but there is no solid authority for either tradition.

In the north-east corner of the garden is a small door leading down to the street through the city wall through which one can easily reach St Augustine's College opposite, and a little further east St Martin's Church. In the last years of the sixth century Queen Bertha used this way to the church and in her memory this small door has always been known as the 'Queningate'.

In the neighbourhood of the garden are some pleasant houses formerly occupied by Canons Residentiary but now leased to the King's School. The most imposing of these is Meister Omers which was built by Prior Chillenden and used to accommodate illustrious guests such as Cardinal Beaufort. This was originally a very large building but much reduced in size after the Reformation and heavily restored in the nineteenth century. It is still very impressive: tall and narrow, and made of flint like many of the domestic buildings of the priory. Close by, with a courtyard in front, is Linacre House whose handsome eighteenth-century façade has been imposed on a much older house behind.

## The Infirmary

Between these houses and the cathedral are the remains of the Norman infirmary of the monks. All that survives of this is a ruined arcade on the south side which must have been part of a large hall of seven bays built in about 1100. Its size reminds us of the number of monks in the community at the time of the great Norman prelates, Lanfranc and Anselm. At the west end of the Infirmary Hall was a charming cloister of the same period, part of which is still intact. At the east end was a chapel, where mass was said, for the sick monks which was much enlarged in the mid-fourteenth century by Prior Hathbrand. The ruins at this end consist of the Romanesque south arcade and its clerestory together with the chancel arch and the fourteenth-century east and north windows that of the north retaining its fine tracery.

In the fifteenth century the south aisle of the hall was blocked up and chambers for the sub-prior built into this area, perhaps because the number of monks had diminished and less space was needed for the infirmary. After the Dissolution this became a private dwelling and was one of the houses assigned in 1541 to the Six Preachers. In 1865 the houses were pulled down and the arches left standing as we see them now. In the post-Reformation period many of the monastic buildings were adapted for the new prebendaries and other clergy. At this time the north arcade was demolished and replaced by the handsome house now used by the cathedral choir boys. Behind stands the somewhat restored Table Hall of the Infirmary built in 1343 for the use of convalescent monks who would eat together here before returning to the ordinary life of the community.

The path between the cathedral and the choir house is known as the Brick Walk, where the ghost of Nell Cook is alleged to walk at 9 pm every Friday night according to the 'Ingoldsby Legends'. From here one can see through the ruined arcade of the infirmary the little Chantry Chapel of King Henry IV, which projects, as if on stilts, from the north ambulatory of the Trinity Chapel. At right angles to the choir aisle stands the Vestiarium or Treasury, its windows still protected against thieves by ancient iron bars. This was built in the middle of the twelfth century when the energetic Prior Wibert was adding to the buildings occupied or used by the monks. There is an open storey below and an upper storey, now used for choir practice, which seems to have been added two hundred years later.

A late medieval doorway leads from the Brick Walk into the little Infirmary Cloister. Looking straight ahead through its Romanesque arches, across the grass, one is confronted by the eastern façade of the modern library which replaced a bombed Victorian predecessor in 1953. On the left is one of the most interesting of all the domestic buildings of the monastery, Prior Wibert's Water Tower. Until 1540 this housed a great bronze tank in which the monks performed their ablutions on their way to the night office of Mattins from the dormitory which stood on the site of the modern library. The lower part of this little building is a Romanesque open storey but Prior Chillenden remodelled the upper storey, which has a mixture of semi-circular and pointed arches inside, and is crowned with a pyramidal cap which makes it conspicuous against the great bulk of the cathedral behind. Although the pipes which linked the lavatorium with the main water system were long ago disconnected, the system is still in working order. Water flows down from the hills of Old Park on the north side of the city, and passes through the settling tanks in the conduit house about a mile away. It is then carried under the main (Military) road and enters the Precincts under the old city at the Forrens courtyard. It sill feeds several taps, one of which is in the arcade just behind the Water Tower.

The new Wolfson Library now runs above the Infirmary Cloister, and perched on top is another small tower with a pyramidal cap. This is all that survives of the Chequer building or the monastic counting house which dated from the time of Prior Eastry (1285 to 1331) and was only demolished in 1868.

### The Green Court

The passage between the Deans' Stairs at the north entrance to the cathedral, and the area known as Green Court on the north side of the Precincts, to which the visitor naturally proceeds at this point, is known as the Dark Entry. There is a magnificent view of the cathedral exterior from here, if one stands with one's back to the lovely little house called the Prior's Gate. This house is usually associated with Prior Sellinge, who is thought to have had it constructed to house his great collection of manuscripts, but it was probably originally built in the time of Prior Chillenden, since the construction of the roof suggests a date much earlier than the late fifteenth century. A feature of this house is a window overlooking the Green Court from which the prior could watch his monks moving among the many buildings around the Green Court which now house the King's School.

On the east side of the Green Court is the imposing façade of the deanery, once part of the prior's lodging. By the later Middle Ages the prior of Christ Church had become a great prelate and lived in a separate house of his own where he would entertain the numerous ecclesiastical and lay magnates, when they came on pilgrimage to the Shrine of St Thomas. The flint tower and building at the south side of the façade is part of the mansion built by Prior Goldstone I, the 'Nova Camera Prioris'. If it seems very large for one Benedictine monk it has to be remembered that this important prelate had a staff of twenty-two servants in 1377 and that by the end of the monastic regime this had been considerably increased. Much of the building perished in a fire in 1569 and the deans, who had taken over this dwelling, had their house repaired in brick as well as stone from the disused monastic buildings. Today the impressive front, sadly much damaged by bombing in 1942, is more eloquent of the presence of Tudor deans than of fifteenth-century priors.

The whole of the north side of the Green Court is occupied by flint buildings which were originally the granary, the brewery and the bakehouse of the monastery. Between the granary (now a canonical residence), and the adjoining offices, all dating from the early fourteenth century, is a handsome Perpendicular gateway leading into a courtyard called the Forrens in which modern brick houses make a pleasant group against the background of the medieval flint wall of the Precincts. Next to the brewery building, now used for classrooms, is a charming small house constructed of a nice medley of flint, stone and brick in 1659 according to a date on the front. The large flint block of buildings next door, now the King's School dining hall, was constructed out of the dwellings of the minor canons in 1938.

Easily the grandest and most famous survival of the Norman period on this side of the Precincts is the staircase built by Prior Wibert. It led to the North Hall, a guest hall, built over arches which still survive, though the school library above is a reconstruction of the mid-nineteenth century. This 'Aula Nova' was built for the accommodation of poor pilgrims who would have slept on the floor, and these with other pilgrims of the 'better sort' would have been met at the Court Gate and sent to their respective lodgings.

This gate, also built by Wibert, adjoins the arches of the vanished North Hall. It is a fine entry to this side of the Precincts, and has some good carving over the arch on the west side. Prior Chillenden built an upper storey over the gate and probably also divided the area underneath into a carriageway and a small postern for foot passengers.

*The Norman staircase in the Green Court.*

The large courtyard linking the Court Gate with the city area of Northgate was once occupied by the Almonry of the Priory which had its own chapel. At the Dissolution this was all taken over by the Crown and subsequently granted by Mary Tudor to Cardinal Pole who left it in his will to the Dean and Chapter for the Cathedral School. In 1859 an extensive range of buildings in flint was constructed on four sides to serve the King's School, a quadrangle known as the Mint Yard because in mid-Tudor times there was a mint here which coined money for the Crown. Leaving the Court Gate and the King's School buildings behind, one can peep through the iron gate in the wall and see the pentise through which pilgrims deemed worthy of better lodgings than the North Hall would be escorted

*A view of the restored cloister arcades on the south side.*

from the Court Gate under shelter. The pentise is a covered way of timber constructed by Prior Chillenden, as is the guest house of flint, Chillenden Chambers, which is now the official residence of the Archdeacon of Canterbury. Part of this house was destroyed by a bomb in 1940, along with the adjoining Larder Gate, but the whole of this large dwelling house has been admirably restored. Remains of the Cellarer's Hall and the great kitchen as well as the Refectory can still be seen in the Archdeacon's garden. In the Water Tower garden there are still remains of the monks' second dormitory and the reredorter or lavatory.

Standing on the south side of the Green Court and looking towards the water tower one is confronted with the same aspect of the cathedral as on the south side of the Precincts: the eye ranges from the western towers and the long roof of the nave, lingering as always, on the central tower and the western transept below and then taking in the choir roof with the Romanesque tower of St Andrew, on this side

*A fifteenth-century boss of Brother John of Sheppey in the cloister vault.*

rising out of the eastern transept with its circular Rose; and then on once more to the Trinity Chapel and Corona. From this point one notes that the domestic buildings were, at Canterbury, on the north side and not on the 'sunny' side as in many Benedictine foundations, perhaps because the city lay mostly on the other side and this was a quieter place for a community, shut away from the busy shops and houses of the citizens as well as the streams of pilgrims.

## The Chapter House

From here we approach the Chapter House and Great Cloister by way of the Prior's Gatehouse and the little Infirmary Cloister, and then through the undercroft of the Priors' Chapel whose pointed arches, with heads carved in the apex of several, are eloquent of the early thirteenth century. The chapel itself was demolished together with the library above, which Archbishop Chichele had given the community in 1440, during the time of the Commonwealth. Within a decade, thanks to a generous gift from Archbishop Juxon (1660-1663) the pleasant red brick building which now houses the Howley-Harrison Library was constructed in its place.

Passing the Deans' Stairs which were built in 'Gothic' style in the latter part of the nineteenth century, the visitor walks through a long tunnel-like passage which runs under the library and between the water tower and the north door of the crypt. All this is Romanesque work, the passage being the sub-vaults of Lanfranc's great dormitory,

*The cloister garth.*

the west wall of which can still be seen in the cloister since it was used in 1868 by H.G. Austin as the west wall of the Cathedral Library. It survived the bombing of 1942 to do duty in the same way for the new Library of 1953.

### The Great Cloister

Now comes the Great Cloister, a rebuilding of an earlier Norman one which was destroyed during the rebuilding of the nave in the late fourteenth century under Yevele. With the rebuilding of its north aisle it was possible to rebuild simultaneously the south cloister alley with a legacy from Archbishop Courtenay who died in 1396. The novices studied here and the stone bench which runs along the outside wall of the nave is pitted with curious hollows which suggests that they played some kind of bagatelle while the outline of soles of shoes suggests another sort of game. There seem to have been carrels or small compartments in this alley separated by timber partitions where studious monks could write and perhaps illuminate; in the later

OPPOSITE: *The door of the Calefactorium in the cloister.*

Middle Ages this side of the cloister must have been glazed to keep out the bitter winds.

The Courtenay Pane, as this wing was called, seems to have used up all the Archbishop's bequest so when the community decided to demolish and rebuild the other three 'panes' they must have launched an appeal for funds since their ordinary financial resources would have been strained to the limit by the amount of work the energetic Chillenden had put in hand. The response was indeed remarkable for it is generally supposed that the profusion of over eight hundred heraldic shields that adorn the vaults of these three alleys represent an enormous subscription list in which the gifts of kings, archbishops, great noblemen and many knights and gentlemen of Kent, as well as other counties, are recorded for posterity. In addition, on the vaulting of the east pane appear the coats of arms of many of the kingdoms and principalities of the first quarter of the fifteenth century, including those of both the Eastern empire and the Holy Roman Empire. In the same alley is a delightful representation of one of the monks, Brother John of Sheppey, who raised a large sum of money for this work, presumably by writing letters begging for aid from his friends and relations in the world outside the convent walls.

In 1935 the Friends of the Cathedral launched an appeal for money with which the shields could be recoloured in their proper tinctures and this enterprise was successfully completed by 1938. To commemorate the royal visit in July 1946 five blank shields in the north pane were carved and painted with the arms of King George VI, Queen Elizabeth and their daughters, Princess Elizabeth and Princess Margaret as well as that of the Dowager Queen Mary. In 1982 the arms of Pope John Paul II, Archbishop Robert Runcie and Charles, Prince of Wales were carved and painted in similar fashion just inside the west door of the cloister to commemorate the Papal visit to Canterbury on 29 May.

The master mason responsible for the designing and building of this new cloister was Yevele's partner Stephen Lote, a Kentish man, who was in charge of the cathedral works from 1400 until his death in 1418. He retained the fine early Gothic doorway and arcade in the wall of the north alley and built, opposite the doorway, which led to the refectory, a lavatorium of two bays which were without mullions so that two large tanks could stand here for the monks to wash on their way from the cathedral for their meals. In the eastern alley is the Romanesque door which led originally into the calefactorium, a chamber where a fire burned in winter time so that the monks could warm themselves in bitter weather. Behind the west wall of the cloister lay the cellarer's quarters, and the 'turn', a hatch through

*The elaborate oak roof of the Chapter House.*

which refreshment could be passed to thirsty monks, can still be seen on the left side of the door which leads to the Archbishop's Palace. It was through this door that St Thomas Becket passed, with the knights in hot pursuit, on the fateful evening of 29 December 1170.

The doorway leading to the transept where the martyrdom took place has undergone several transformations since that event. Originally a simple Romanesque archway, this principal entrance to the Church for the monks was remodelled in the early English Gothic style as a richly carved and coloured doorway with niches on either side. Some two hundred years later, Lote's rebuilding of the whole cloister unfortunately demanded the insertion of a stone vault in place of the wooden Norman roof. This with the shafts that supported it and a new door case of the fifteenth century, has ruined the sumptuous effect of the original thirteenth-century entrance to the transept which can still be discerned showing through the later alterations. In between the Martyrdom Transept doorway and the Chapter House is the Slype, a narrow passage leading to the area behind the east end of the Lady Chapel and the Chapter House.

A visit to the Chapter House makes an excellent conclusion to the study of the monastic buildings. The largest of its kind in England, it was rebuilt by Prior Eastry in 1304, its Romanesque predecessor most likely being a rectangle of modest proportions like other Norman Chapter Houses which survive unaltered as at Bristol and Gloucester. Prior Eastry kept the rectangular shape but created a huge hall, nearly a hundred feet in length, with a noble doorway, a double stone seat for the monks running round the sides with an arcade behind, and at the east end a throne-like seat for the prior, or the archbishop when he was present. There are also seats for the obedientiaries or heads of departments on either side of the prior. Chillenden carried out a characteristic remodelling early in the fifteenth century and it is to this period that we owe the magnificent timber roof of gilded and coloured Irish bog oak, the profusion of heraldry on the roof and walls, the large east and west windows, and the curious blank windows on the north side where the dormitory wall of Lanfranc's day meets the Chapter House of Eastry and Chillenden.

Coming out into the cloister a glance at the modern tombstones of archbishops and deans may be of interest to students of monumental calligraphy. The inscriptions on the slab which covers the remains of Archbishop Frederick Temple were designed and carved by Eric Gill in 1904, who also designed that for Dean 'Dick' Sheppard in 1938. More recently the slab over the grave of Dean Hewlett Johnson was carved by the local sculptor, W.G. Day after the Dean's death in 1966. A large memorial tablet on the west wall of the cloister records the names of those whose cremated remains lie under the grass of the Garth; this is the work of Ralph Beyer, 1979. Most recent of additions is an oval tablet beside the calefactorium door leading to the modern cathedral library. This is the work of David Kindersley (1982) in memory of Dr. William Urry, most learned of modern historians of the cathedral and its archivist and librarian for many years. From this point it is convenient to return along the dormitory passage to the north door of the crypt, and entering there to begin a study of the interior architecture of the cathedral.

# Chapter Three

# A WALK AROUND THE CATHEDRAL INTERIOR

THE CRYPT or undercroft is the best starting point for a chronological walk around the building studying the development of the various styles of medieval ecclesiastical architecture. Lanfranc's church ended at the west wall of the crypt inside the Silver Treasury. From this wall stretches the crypt, which was built under the direction of the great Prior Ernulf from 1096 onwards. Away to the east it culminates in the lovel Chapel of Our Lady to whom the whole crypt was dedicated and which is still known as Our Lady Undercroft. In the middle of this wall there seems to have been an entrance door linking the crypt with the original nave and crossing. On either side, set into the wall, is a simple shaft with a plain capital and these with two others in the same wall belong to Lanfranc's church.

### The Western Crypt

From the west wall the Romanesque arches which support the simple stone roof march eastwards towards the distant sanctuary of Our Lady Undercroft. These arches, resting on a forest of twenty-two free-standing columns, are arranged in pairs and the carvings of the capitals and columns alike are brilliantly executed, particularly since they were all reputedly carved with an axe.

The usual plan seems to have been for the capital to be carved and the shaft to be left plain, alternating with a carved shaft and plain capital, but here and there the scheme seems to have broken down, as if the masons who were set to carve by the designer were not clear about his intentions and had gone too far to alter what they had done when the mistakes were discovered. This suggests that the carving was done on the spot when the pillars were in place. While the shafts are carved with fluting or patterns of various kinds, the most elaborate being in the chapels of St Gabriel and the Holy Innocents, the capitals,

ABOVE: *Romanesque carved capitals in the crypt.*

mostly carved on all four sides, have weird and wonderful figures and scenes which do not seem to have any religious significance at all: a man on horseback, a lion, a man fighting with a beast of some kind, a juggler with a man on his head and creatures which seem to resemble dragons locked in combat. St Bernard of Clairvaux, the great monastic reformer, denounced this kind of decoration in a famous piece of invective, which suggests it was not uncommon in Benedictine churches in France: 'What is the meaning of these ridiculous monsters, of that deformed beauty, that beautiful deformity, before the eyes of the brethren when reading? Good God! if we are not ashamed of these absurdities, why do we not grieve at the cost of them?'

The western crypt with its associations with St Anselm and Prior Ernulf has few equals in the Christian world for size and dignity. It is in fact a grand Romanesque church, partly below ground level, which allows light to penetrate in a wonderfully mysterious way from the numerous windows in the exterior walls. The central nave and side aisles are separated from the outer processional aisles by an arcade of massive piers which sweeps right round the east end, forming an apsidal termination, which is concealed from the west end viewer by the lovely fourteenth-century screens enclosing the sanctuary area. Leading out of the main crypt are the transepts with double chapels, each of which has an apse in which the altar is set. These transepts are the undercroft of the eastern transepts of the main church above. A 'vice' or staircase of the same date as the crypt leads up to the storey above and then passes up to the Romanesque towers of St Andrew and St Anselm. Further east still are the radiating chapels leading out of

BELOW: *The Romanesque western crypt, started in Anselm's time.*

**The Cathedral Crypt**

**Key**
1  Silver Treasury
2  St Nicholas and St Mary Magdelen's Chapels
3  Huguenot Church (Black Prince's Chantry)
4  Holy Innocents Chapel
5  Chapel of Our Lady Undercroft
6  St Gabriel's Chapel
7  Jesus Chapel
8  Eastern Crypt
9  Western Crypt

the processional path as it begins to turn round the east end. These chapels, also, have contemporary staircases leading to the chapels above and the chambers over them.

The first burial place of St Thomas of Canterbury appears to have been behind the apse, more or less under the Sanctuary and High Altar of the church above. Here Henry II would have performed his penance and the first pilgrims come to venerate the martyr's body and to pray. The crypt would have ended here with an eastern chapel dedicated to St Augustine. These chapels were demolished when the eastern crypt was built, c. 1180, as an extension in the Transitional Gothic style to make a feretory area where the tomb of St Thomas could be placed allowing plenty of space for the pilgrims whose numbers increased rapidly in the decades that followed the martyrdom.

No doubt there would have been many side altars in the crypt in the pre-Reformation times when every monk in priests' orders was accustomed to say mass every day. After the Dissolution, when other ideas prevailed about the priesthood and the eucharist, all these altars would have been swept away. In 1575 the western crypt became the meeting house for the flood of Huguenot refugees, while the eastern crypt was walled off to become a coal cellar for the members of the reformed chapter. The rather crude paintings which appear all over the vault of this western crypt representing the crown of thorns and roses may date from this period. A richly decorative note is provided by the screens around the Lady Altar. These are tabernacle work and it has been suggested that the cathedral owed this as well as the painted shields and other decorations here to the generosity of Lady Mohun of Dunster whose fourteenth-century tomb by the south side of the chapel is of the same period as the screens.

The chapels in the north transept are dedicated to St Nicholas and St Mary Magdalene. They have been refurnished in the last half century and are in regular use for the morning celebrations of Holy Communion which are held in a different chapel of the cathedral each day of the week. The transept has two curious Gothic features which catch the eye in the austere Romanesque setting: one is a slab on the floor which has a floriated cross carved upon it, similar to the covering of the coffin-like tomb of Archbishop Stephen Langton in St Michael's Chapel. It may well have come from some destroyed thirteenth-century tomb since it does not appear to cover a grave of any kind. The other curiosity is the central octagonal column which supports the vault of the transept and has a number of fragmented crockets sprouting from it which may be a substitution of the early Gothic period c. 1175.

*The Icon of the Annunciation from St Gabriel's Chapel.*

The Chapel of the Holy Innocents has two notable columns and these are unusual in having both shafts and capitals carved. The capital of the pillar which supports the arches facing the sanctuary is ornamented with scroll and leaf patterns, and the shaft is carved with an overlapping leaf or scale design. The western pillar has what appear to be dragons on two sides and elaborately floral designs on the other two; its shaft is carved with a fluted design. In the fifteenth century the apse was replaced with a square Perpendicular window in the east wall and its counterpart, St Gabriel's Chapel opposite, had its east wall squared off likewise, but without a window. In 1985 a beautiful modern icon, the work of Brother Luke of the Benedictine Abbey of Chevtogne was placed on this wall in memory of Hewlett and Noel Johnson. The wall paintings in this chapel are described elsewhere (see p. 163).

The carvings on the capitals of the pillars which support the roof of this chapel are a very impressive example of Romanesque art of the twelfth century. That in the middle, linking the two naves, has a line pattern on the shaft and each of the four sides of the capital has carvings of fantastic beasts playing antique musical instruments or dancing in the utmost abandon. Until the year 1879 admission to the sanctuary of this chapel was by a tiny hole in the wall since the space between the arches was walled in. Then a doorway was made into the sanctuary area, and a few years after the ending of the Second World War, the wall was demolished and much painting discovered in the soffit of the twin arches. We owe the preservation of the paintings to the blocking up of the sanctuary. The wall was inserted early in the medieval period either for structural reasons, because the weight of St Anselm's Chapel above was proving too heavy for this area below, or because the monks needed some place in which to keep valuables and treasures during the troubled half century which followed the martyrdom of St Thomas and culminated in their exile to St Omer in the reign of King John.

The southern transept to the west of this chapel has been for the last century the Huguenot Church, since the community moved out of the main crypt. Today it presents the appearance of a Calvinistic place of worship with a prominent pulpit and a small communion table. The original Romanesque work here would have been a replica of the other transept opposite with two apsidal chapels and a dividing wall.

As the price of his dispensation for permission to marry his cousin Joan, the Fair Maid of Kent, the Black Prince established a chantry here with two altars where priests would pray for ever for the souls of himself and his wife. In 1363 the work was set in hand for the transformation of this severe little transept into a rich chantry of early Perpendicular Gothic. Since Henry Yevele had been working for the Prince since 1357 and was described as his mason in 1359, he may have been the architect charged with the task of clothing the Norman piers with new work. The clustered shafts and lovely lierne vaults with their handsome bosses are a foretaste of splendours to come in the nave and cloister. The bosses include coats of arms of the Prince and his royal father, a portrait usually identified as his wife Joan, the sacramental 'pelican in her piety' and Samson smiting the Philistines with the jawbone of an ass, usually supposed to symbolize the Prince's great victories over the huge French armies at Crécy and Poitiers. Perpendicular windows were inserted in the apses about this time,

63

*A fourteenth-century boss from the Black Prince's Chantry in the crypt.*

and, in recent years, the Gothic 'skin' has been removed in two places in the southern apse to show Romanesque capitals inside.

## The Eastern Crypt

Walking east, we come to the threshold of the crypt of William the Englishman and notice in the ambulatory, behind the altar of Our Lady Undercroft, two huge columns which are thought to have been brought here by William of Sens to support the piers of the new choir above and clearly belong to the earlier church. In the south aisle of the Gothic crypt can be seen two free-standing pillars which do not belong to the cathedral. They were formerly part of the chancel screen of the Saxon church of Reculver and are monoliths, twenty feet high, possibly dating from the seventh century. Fragments of a great cross of the same date, which stood in front of the screen, are preserved in the cathedral but are not at present on exhibition. Light pours in through the lancet windows, six on each side though one is now blocked, and a ribbed vault rests on eight coupled columns which sweep around the crypt in a great semi-circle.

## The Jesus Chapel

At the east end, beyond the ambulatory, is the Jesus Chapel which is the undercroft of the Corona. This is a lovely Gothic apse with a vaulted roof sprinkled with painted letters, M and I crowned, whose

*The Romanesque diaper wall in the Martyrdom Transept.*

ribs meet in a richly carved boss recently painted in red and gold. In the centre of the main crypt are two columns of Purbeck marble supporting the vault; between these lay the tomb of St Thomas, a plain marble edifice with holes in the sides, which is portrayed many times over in the Miracle Windows of the Trinity Chapel above. William the Englishman was in charge of the work by the time the old east end of the crypt was demolished, and the new crypt seems to have been built in not much more than two years, work beginning in 1179 and being completed in 1181. The tomb of the martyr, which had been boarded over during building operations, was then moved into the centre (from its first resting place behind the altar of Our Lady Undercroft) where it lay for nearly forty years. It is clear that this was not intended to be the final resting place of the martyr for work was begun immediately after its completion, on the Trinity Chapel which was to become one of the most splendid shrine chapels in Europe. However, the eastern crypt was certainly a very impressive place for pilgrims to visit at this stage in the development of the cult of St Thomas, and must have impressed all who saw it by its novel arcade in Transitional Gothic style, the western arches being semi-circular as if looking back to the Romanesque tradition, while the arches towards the east and the deeply recessed windows in the exterior walls are typically Gothic in their pointed character. High up in the west wall over the entrance arch are two windows which light a watching

## Plan of the Cathedral

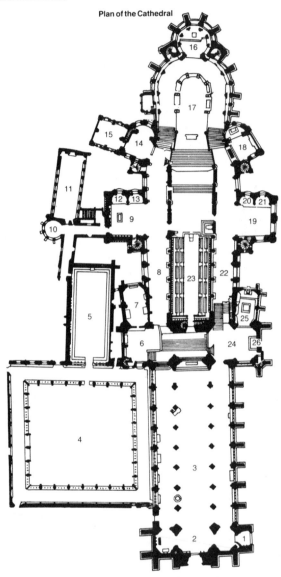

**Key**

1  South-West Door
2  West Door
3  Nave
4  Cloisters
5  Chapter House
6  North-West Transept or Martyrdom Transept
7  Lady Chapel
8  North Choir Aisle
9  North-East Transept
10  Water Tower
11  Howley-Harrison Library
12  St Martin's Chapel
13  St Stephen's Chapel
14  St Andrew's Chapel
15  Treasury or Vestiarium
16  Corona
17  Trinity Chapel
18  St Anselm's Chapel
19  South-East Transept
20  St John's Chapel
21  St Gregory's Chapel
22  South Choir Aisle
23  Choir
24  South-West Transept
25  St Michael's Chapel or Holland Chapel
26  South Door

chamber under the High Altar. From here the monks could keep a permanent eye on their greatest treasure, the martyr's body in its marble tomb below.

Returning through the crypt and ascending the staircase to the Martyrdom Transept from the north ambulatory one passes through the Norman doorway which leads up through contemporary walls decorated with a diaper pattern. Concealed within the rich covering of the Perpendicular walls of the transept, which was erected between 1448 and 1468, is a good deal of the stone-work of Lanfranc's church, the small door in the north-west corner leading to the only 'vice' or staircase which survives from his time.

Climbing the steps that lead from the Martyrdom Transept to the pulpitum screen one becomes aware of one of the most unusual and impressive features of the interior of the cathedral: the gradual rise in levels from the floor of the nave to the Trinity Chapel, which is some twenty-five feet (eight metres) above ground level. This is, of course, due to the presence of the two crypts of different height underneath the eastern arm of the church. At some time after the fire of 1174, it must have been decided to raise the vaulted roof of the eastern crypt considerably above that of the Romanesque Crypt, thus lifting the Trinity Chapel and the Shrine, which was to be placed in a dominating position in its centre, high above the choir. From the west door of the choir one can look back to the nave below and then turn east and see the steps rising, first to the platform on which the High Altar stands, and then a further flight to the level of the chapel floor with the Marble Chair of the Primates providing a link between altar and shrine in medieval times.

## The Choir

The monastic choir was rebuilt according to the design of William of Sens, work beginning in the year that followed the fire, with the erection of eight pillars, alternately octagonal and cylindrical. Four were set up in 1175 and two more in each of the following years. Here, as in the rest of the church, the material was Caen limestone, imported by water from Normandy, brought by barge to the port of Fordwich two miles or so away and then unloaded and borne to the Cathedral Precincts by waggons. Skilled carvers, possibly French, using the chisel rather than the axe went to work on the capitals of the choir pillars, creating lovely and delicate foliated designs with water leaves, berries and grapes. A novel form of ornamentation was provided by the introduction of brown shafts which contrasted well with the Caen limestone. These are made of marble from the Isle of Purbeck in Dorset: it seems most likely that this would have been

*'The junction of the axe and the chisel' in the south ambulatory.*

brought by water around the south coast and up the River Stour to Fordwich like the Caen stone. The marble shafts are used in the triforium all round the choir and transepts as well as the Trinity Chapel, and provide a link with the main arcades. They are also used in the piers of the crossing where they run the whole length of each pier. While they were introduced by the French master mason they obviously appealed to his successor, William the Englishman, who took his place in 1178. Another attractive feature of the new choir was the bosses or key stones which bound together the ribs in the stone vaulting both of the choir and the ambulatories. The finest of these is to be seen in the main crossing vault. It represents the Lamb and Flag, a symbol of the Resurrection, particularly appropriately placed at the centre of Christ Church Cathedral.

By Easter 1180 the choir of the monks was sufficiently complete for the community to hold its festival there, so we can assume that the vaulting was in position and perhaps some of the glass of the clerestory as well. Gervase has left us a detailed account of this great event in the life of the priory, and of the gradual rebuilding of the

OPPOSITE: *The vaulting of the Trinity Chapel.*

choir followed by the building of the presbytery. A visit to the choir ambulatories shows how much of the Romanesque church it was possible to retain, for the old arcading runs right round both inside and outside, as far as the steps that lead to the new Shrine Chapel. No doubt at the request of the monks, the two architects agreed to retain the two Norman Chapels of St Anselm and St Andrew which necessitated bending the ambulatories around creating a curious 'wasp waist' effect, which often puzzles the student. By 1184 work on the Trinity Chapel was ready to go ahead. The main choir and presbytery as well as the transepts with their two rose windows in position would have been complete, and the triforia and clerestory finished also. A curious sight can be seen in the south ambulatory just west of the crossing where a mason has carved a pointed arch with the 'dog tooth' moulding into the Romanesque arcade. This was a new kind of ornamentation which occurs here from now onwards and became popular all over England.

During the rebuilding, the stained glass artists would have been putting in the great series of genealogical figures all round the choir and transepts, and the monks would have been planning the series of twelve Bible Windows which followed in both ambulatories and transepts.

Walking along the south ambulatory of the choir to the transept one passes the pillars of the presbytery which were set in position while William of Sens was still in charge. It was while the work of turning the vault over the High Altar was in hand that he fell from the scaffolding and it was at this stage that William the Englishman took over. To him we owe the completion of the church from the Pilgrim Steps to Trinity Chapel and the Corona. Looking through the beautiful Romanesque arch of the Chapel of St Anselm into the mysterious Gothic areas that stretch away to the west of the choir, one can imagine the monk Gervase growing ever more excited as he saw unimaginable splendours taking shape before his eyes during the work of construction. Above the simple rib vault of the chapel is a commodious chamber which gives access to a little gallery overlooking the mosaic pavement and western end of the Trinity Chapel. The view of the shrine from here is very limited, so it is unlikely that this was another watching chamber. It is more probably one of a series of chambers constructed in Norman times which were used for storage purposes, as is still the case today.

## The Trinity Chapel

Sixteen steps lead up to the Trinity Chapel with its evocative empty space where the shrine once stood, brilliant with its golden-

*Twelfth-century vaulting of the Corona.*

plated coffin-chest. The chapel, with its lovely windows, mosaic pavement and double piers of pinkish Purbeck marble with delicately carved capitals, is a master work of English architecture which inspired many such shrine chapels in England and elsewhere in years to come. The spaces between the pillars round the inner chapel were filled at a later stage with noble tombs. Around these runs the ambulatory from which one passes into the Corona with a vaulted roof, tall windows and yet more Purbeck marble shafts and dog tooth ornamentation. Inside, the unfinished exterior is not apparent. It seems, somehow, to be exactly the right termination of this great

71

*Encaustic tiles from the Jesus Chapel in the eastern crypt.*

church. Today its former association with the relic of St Thomas is appropriately replaced by the modern rededication to the saints and martyrs of our own time. It has a great atmosphere of devotion as, once again, votive candles burn at its entrance and pilgrims of many languages come to pray before its altar whose frontal is embroidered with the words of T.S. Eliot, 'the blood of Thy Martyrs and Saints shall enrich the earth, shall create the Holy Places.'

Passing down the ambulatory from the Corona to the north range of Pilgrim Steps one finds on the right hand side, opposite the royal tomb of Henry IV and his Queen Joan, the lovely little chantry which they founded and dedicated to the royal saint Edward the Confessor.

Dedicated in 1439, two years after the death of Queen Joan, it is built between the buttresses of the Trinity Chapel and is entered by a fine oak screen. The chapel, which can only hold a handful of people at any time, is protected by iron bars on the ambulatory side and is roofed with a very early example of a fan vault. It rests on pillars outside and its windows look over the infirmary ruins.

Near the foot of the Pilgrim Steps is the watching chamber of the crypt, known today as the 'Wax Chamber'. This lies under the platform where the Marble Chair of the Primates stands. The chamber itself is low pitched with a floor of encaustic tiles and a quadripartite vault with some dogtooth ornament and uncarved bosses.

Standing outside St Andrew's Chapel it is possible to see how the great parclose screen runs on either side of the monastic choir. This fine piece of early fourteenth-century work is perhaps Prior Eastry's most enduring memorial. It originally comprised the pulpitum which was then covered by the present Screen of the Six Kings in the early years of the fifteenth century, on the nave side. Not very long after its erection the intrusion of archiepiscopal tombs on either side of the presbytery gradually eliminated large sections of the screen. One of these sections, which ran between the tombs of Archbishop Chichele and Bourchier, was removed in favour of the cenotaph of Archbishop Howley in the middle of the nineteenth century and now forms the screen of St Andrew's Chapel. Eastry's screen is adorned in its upper areas with open windows (now glazed) and a battlemented parapet. Handsome doorways admit to the presbytery on north and south sides.

St Andrew's Chapel has Romanesque arcades like its fellow opposite and two chambers above of later date. One of these is used for storage and the other for choir rehearsals. A delightful little fourteenth-century piscina remains on the east side of the chapel but no altar stands here now and the chapel is, in fact, a vestibule to the Vestiarium or Treasury which has been the vestry of the dean and canons for generations. Approached through a massive medieval wooden door with three locks, the Vestiarium itself has a splendid vault with eight ribs which meet in a keystone or boss carved with lions' heads in a circle. The capitals of the pillars on which the vault rests are carved with grotesque human heads. The building dates from the time of Prior Wibert c. 1153 and, with its barred windows and four-square interior set over an open undercroft, ranks with the Water Tower as a major piece of construction which gives Wibert a place among the great building priors of Christ Church.

A little further west along the ambulatory, is a recess in the wall

*The piscina from St Andrew's Chapel*

which was once the Easter Sepulchre where the Reserved Host and Altar Cross would have rested between Maundy Thursday and the Vigil ceremonies of Easter Day. In 1541 the archives record the making of a wooden desk in this recess to which Cranmer's Bible was chained for all to read, a reminder that with the Reformation the dramatic ceremonies of the medieval church gave way to the reading of the Scriptures and expository sermons as the usual means of teaching the Faith.

## The North East Transept

A curious link with monastic times can be seen in the north-east transept, alongside which was originally constructed the Prior's Chapel, destroyed under the Commonwealth. In the north wall of the transept are three lancets which are hagioscopes or squints through which the priors could see into the transept and presbytery without being seen. A fourth aperture concealed in a splay of a

*The boss in the vaulting of the Norman Vestiarium or Treasury.*

window in the wall commands a view of the apsidal chapels of St Martin and St Stephen so that the prior could see the Elevation of the Host when Mass was being said there.

A late medieval doorway in the north wall of the transept leads straight into a passage which the monks used at night on their way from the dormitory into the cathedral for the office of Mattins. They would pause to wash their hands and faces in the great tank in the upper part of the adjoining Water Tower. The passage is set over a little Romanesque arcade below but in its present form owes much to a remodelling of Chillenden's time. This also extended to the Water Tower itself, whose conical roof with its lead covering and fifteenth-century windows fits quite happily on top of the Romanesque substructure. In recent years two twelfth-century windows have been uncovered as part of the restoration of the upper part of the tower. A magnificent thirteenth-century doorway, which faces down the passage to the library is all that has survived of the Prior's Chapel.

Returning to the choir and walking down to the west door the small galleries on each side of the ambulatories catch the eye with their attractive stained glass windows and marble shafts. Access to these, as to the triforium and the clerestory above, is obtained from doors in the eastern transepts. The stairs inside ultimately lead up to the towers of St Andrew and St Anselm. The dim religious light of the choir and its dark Victorian stallwork has been enlivened recently by the provision of a number of embroidered cushions for the seats and backstalls, worked by ladies of the Friends of the Cathedral. These are embroidered with the coats of arms of archbishops, deans and archdeacons of Canterbury, and were placed in position in December 1985.

## The Nave

At this point the visitor should leave the choir and walk straight down the nave to stand at the west doors and look eastwards where the full glory of the great Perpendicular building stretches before him. By visiting the great Benedictine churches of Gloucester, Tewkesbury and Durham where the Romanesque naves have survived, intact, to the present day one can imagine what the effect must have been on entering the nave of Canterbury down to the year 1370. But no one who is familiar with the Perpendicular glories of the cathedral today would really regret the demolition of Lanfranc's nave. This took place in 1377, the cost being borne by Archbishop Simon of Sudbury whose generosity is commemorated by the appearance of his coat of arms on either side of the north door of the new building as well as on the vaulting of the main arcade. Only the west towers and crossing tower were left standing. In Sudbury's lifetime a lot of work was done on the side aisles, the archbishop contributing something like £2000 before his murder. Over the next ten years work went on gradually. Richard II and other magnates, encouraged by the new archbishop, William Courtenay, contributed a thousand marks.

The nave was completed in the first years of the fifteenth century, by which time the architect Henry Yevele was dead, so much of the credit for the final stages of the work must rest with the energetic Prior Chillenden who dominated the affairs of the priory from his election in 1391 until his death in 1411. Apart from its tall piers and lofty arcades there are some noticeable features of this work. One is the absence of a triforium which is replaced by a panelled wall, behind which run the passages over the aisle vaults linking the central with

OPPOSITE: *A pier in the nave.*

the south-west bell tower. Next is the elaborate lierne vault, in which many ribs are linked together in the central nave and then the great range of windows in the side walls which flood the building with light, accentuated doubtless by the destruction of the stained glass by seventeenth-century iconoclasts. Another novelty is the profusion of coats of arms which first began to appear here, as all over England, in the last half of the fourteenth century, providing both a colourful and meaningful form of decoration in cathedrals and parish churches alike.

A short way up the nave is a great strainer arch which stretches over the nave altar of Holy Cross and is one of several such arches inserted in the time of Prior Goldstone II who was in office from 1495 to 1517. In his time two great medieval works, the central tower and the Christ Church Gate were completed. The strainers were necessary because of the great weight of the new tower on the piers of the crossing. Wastell, the architect of the tower, must have devised the attractive quatrefoil design which makes the strainers decorative as well as functional. The familiar rebus of Prior Goldstone, three gold stones on a blue ground, appears on the great western strainer along with his motto carved in stone, 'Non nobis, Domine, non nobis'.

At the end of the nave rises the great flight of steps which lead into the choir and here one is confronted by the pulpitum screen erected in Chillenden's day. It acts both as a support to the tower above and as a superb 'backcloth' to the many festival services held nowadays in the nave. It is usually known as the Screen of the Six Kings, since the statues, which stand in tall niches looking west, are all in royal robes and splendid crowns. Usually thought to be Henry V, Richard II and Ethelbert on the left side of the door and Edward the Confessor, Henry IV and Henry VI on the right hand side, they have been attributed to a well known sculptor, John Massingham III, who had Canterbury connections. They may have been carved from life in the case of the Plantagenet sovereigns, all of whom visited the cathedral on pilgrimage at different times in their reigns. The screen, which covers Eastry's older one, is a very rich affair with a frieze of angels across the front. It originally had figures of the twelve apostles and 'twelve martyred saints' in the other niches but these were destroyed during the Civil War.

At this point, having climbed the great flight of steps, one can look up into the tower, the masterpiece of John Wastell, and admire the famous fan vault with the arms of King Henry VII, Prior Goldstone II

OPPOSITE: *The great strainer arch in the nave from the pulpitum screen.*

and the two archbishops, John Morton and William Warham, in whose time the mighty work was begun, continued and so gloriously brought to completion. Inside the tower is a gallery which runs right round, providing doors on each of its four sides to the spaces or voids over the roof of nave, choir, and transepts.

In the centre of the vault is a circular trapdoor, painted with the arms of the priory, (still borne by the post-Reformation chapter), which is raised by a wooden crane in a chamber above the actual vault. In the main part of the tower, where the vast number of Tudor bricks form the walls unclothed with Caen stone, stands the great wheel or treadmill, one of three still surviving in medieval English churches. Its woodwork has been much renewed over the centuries, and it is no longer in use, a hand operated windlass having recently taken its place. At the top of the steps under the tower is a stone seat built into the south wall where the Ostiarius, a monastic official, would sit as guardian of the choir gate during services. A passage runs under the platform linking the two transepts so that pilgrims could pass from one to the other without having to traverse the area in front of the pulpitum screen.

From the steps one can look at the great windows of both transepts in turn, as well as the west window of the nave, and enjoy the brilliant effect of these huge areas of glass which are one of the glories of the cathedral. Noticeable here, too, is the fact that the strainer arches which support the tower to the west and south are missing on the north side, perhaps because the monks were reluctant to hide their great new Royal Window, the gift of Edward IV in 1482.

The rebuilding of the south-west transept was finished by 1430, and work began in 1437 on the rebuilding of St Michael's Chapel and the Chapel of All Saints above it. By this time Thomas Mapilton, who was master mason of cathedral works during the rebuilding of the south transept had retired in favour of Richard Beke who would have designed these two chapels. Since he held office from 1432 to 1458 he probably designed the rebuilding of the north-west transept and the Lady Chapel by the Martyrdom Transept. These transepts and chapels were the last major works of pre-Reformation days other than the central tower which binds all together. St Michael's Chapel, designed as a mausoleum for Lady Margaret Holland and her two husbands, is a rich and impressive piece of mid-fifteenth-century work completed by the end of 1439, a few days before the death of the great lady. On the lierne vault are shields commemorating her

OPPOSITE: *The pulpitum screen.*

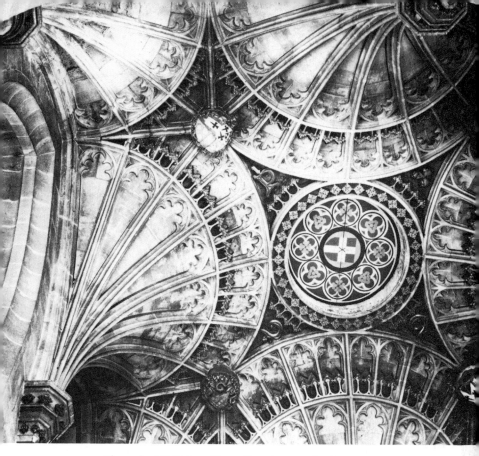

*The vault of Bell Harry Tower from clerestorey level.*

alliances with the families of Beaufort and Plantagenet. The two storey plan was preserved here and a spacious, well-lit Chapel of All Saints was constructed above St Michael's Chapel. Reached by a flight of stairs in the wall of the south ambulatory, the most memorable feature of the chapel is the vaulting which has three bosses carved with cowled heads of the priors of the first forty years of the century: Prior Chillenden, Prior Wodensburgh, his successor, and Prior Molash. (All these names are those of Kentish villages within a few miles of Canterbury which suggests that the Benedictine Priory tended to draw its monks from the surrounding countryside.)

*Three kings from the pulpitum screen: from left to right Edward the Confessor, Henry IV and Henry VI.*

83

*Vault of Bell Harry Tower.*

*The treadmill from Bell Harry Tower.*

The Martyrdom Transept with its associations with St Thomas and the most dramatic incident in the history of the cathedral was the last part of the western arm of the church to be rebuilt, as if the monastic chapter was reluctant to alter a part of their beloved building with such historic associations. Any such reluctance was eventually overcome and work was completed by the end of the reign of Edward IV with the insertion of the glass in the great north window. The plan adopted in the opposite transept of demolishing two Romanesque chapels, situated one on top of another, and rebuilding them in the new style was not followed here. Instead a most beautiful chapel dedicated to the Assumption of our Lady and St Benedict was constructed during the early years of Prior Goldstone and dedicated

85

*Prior Molash's head in All Saints Chapel.*

in 1455. Its roof is an early example of fan vaulting and gains in height with the absence of the chapel above. Entering through a lovely stone screen one is immediately attracted by the richness of the carving; empty niches for statues all round the sanctuary area with tall pinnacled canopies; a large east window of five lights with an elaborately carved border of leaves; and a charming frieze of angels holding scrolls running underneath the east window. The central one, recently brought to light during a restoration, still shows some traces of colour and on the scroll are the words, *'Gloria tua'*. Originally there seem to have been stalls for monks against the side walls. These have long gone and in the south wall can be seen a fragment of a Romanesque pillar, all that remains of the former chapel. From this quiet corner of the cathedral, an ideal place for prayer and meditation, we can proceed to examine the many windows of early Gothic glass which makes Canterbury unique among English churches.

# Chapter Four

# THE STAINED GLASS

T HE GREAT COLLECTION of early Gothic glass which still fills many of the windows of the cathedral must be reckoned by any standards to be one of the most outstanding treasures of medieval art still surviving in this country. The fire of 1174 would have destroyed any earlier glass in the eastern part of the Romanesque cathedral. William of Sens, who directed the rebuilding of the choir probably brought a band of artists and glaziers over from France, where the art and craft of stained glass was beginning to be seen in all its early glory in cathedrals like Chartres and Le Mans, to design and make Canterbury's stained glass, though it is doubtful whether he would have seen many of the windows completed. As we shall see the earliest glass to survive dates from 1178 and the latest windows of this period cannot be much later than 1220, so for at least forty years the glaziers must have been at work intermittently filling the windows of the choir and its ambulatories as well as the eastern transepts, Trinity Chapel and Corona with richly coloured figures and scenes from Holy Scripture and the lives of the saints.

The early Gothic glass of Canterbury Cathedral differs from any other collections that have come down to us from England or France because it is a carefully planned scheme teaching the Christian faith through pictures in glass.

Though a great deal of glass has disappeared we can detect three different areas of related teaching, all intended to expound the mighty works of God revealed in the Incarnation of Our Lord Jesus Christ and in the history of his Church. First of all is the series of splendid figures dating from the last quarter of the twelfth century which filled the clerestory of the choir running in a great band below the high vault, taking in the eastern transepts and the apsidal end of the Trinity Chapel. These figures were intended to form a family tree based on the genealogy in St Luke's Gospel, which begins with Adam and ends with Christ thus emphasizing the fact that Jesus Christ was perfect Man and Perfect God. Of this series, which originally numbered some eighty-eight figures, there are still forty-five to be seen in the cathedral in various places.

A second cycle of Biblical subjects dating from around 1200 AD was intended to fill the windows of the choir ambulatory and transepts, six on the north side and six on the south. These were linked together by the great circular windows in the gables of the transepts symbolizing, in the north gable the Old Testament and, in the south window opposite, the New. Only two of these Bible Windows survive from the original twelve but there is a thirteenth in the Corona.

The teaching scheme was concluded by a number of windows with scenes from the lives of the saints after whom the four apsidal chapels of the transepts were dedicated. These were St Martin and St Stephen in the north transept and St John the Evangelist and St Gregory the Great in the south. Scarcely any of the glass survives in these chapels but this is more than atoned for by a splendid series of windows dating from the first quarter of the thirteenth century. In these the life and the miracles of St Thomas (posthumous) are illustrated to make the point that the power of the Holy Spirit was evident not only in the lives and works of the Biblical Saints but of those in every age since Pentecost, and pre-eminently in the life of St Thomas so recently murdered in this very cathedral and canonized in the memory of so many still alive. These Miracle Windows fill five windows in the north ambulatory of the shrine chapel and three on the opposite side. Though much restored, they are still among the most brilliant and enjoyable of all early Gothic glass.

## The Great West Window

A tour of the cathedral glass may best begin at the bottom of the nave looking up at the great west window. This window was inserted at the very beginning of the fifteenth century and the tracery work helps to date it for it is contemporary with the stonework. The shields of arms must have been inserted between 1394 when Richard II's beloved Queen Anne of Bohemia died and 1399 when he was deposed. Queen Anne's arms appear just below those of her Royal husband while those of his second wife, the little Isabella of France (whom he married in 1396) appear on the opposite side. At the top of the tracery lights are six prophets who wear hats to distinguish them from a number of apostles who are haloed in the row below. This was a favourite subject throughout the Middle Ages and a complete set of

OPPOSITE: *A king from the Corona window (1861).*

apostles including St Matthias appear in the bottom row of the tracery.

If these figures all date from the beginning of the century, the eight figures of kings in royal robes and crowns that fill the main lights below would appear to be anything up to forty years later. They are all that survive from a series of twenty-one figures of the kings of England from Canute to Henry VI that once filled these lights and were presumably smashed by the Puritans in 1642 who must also have deprived posterity of all the fifteenth-century glass in the aisles of the nave. The kings are not named but Bernard Rackham suggests that they may be Canute, William I, Harold (Godwinson) II, Edward the Confessor, William II, Henry I and Stephen while the solitary figure in the second row may be Henry III. The lights on either side of this monarch are filled with fifteenth-century coats of arms including those of archbishops connected with the cathedral.

Small figures of archbishops and Apostles of the same date were brought here from other parts of the building in the last decade of the eighteenth century when the vesturer of the cathedral, William Burgys, was commissioned by Dean Powys and his Chapter to fill the blank spaces in this window and its fellow in the south-west transept with glass from elsewhere. The vesturer moved a number of the great genealogical figures from the clerestory of the choir placing thirteen of them in the lower lights of this window and twenty-four in the south-west transept. In the second row of lights there are from left to right Jeconias, Obed and Rehoboam, and then Abia, Jesse and Salathiel. Fifteenth-century coats of arms run along the top and bottom of the lowest range of lights which are dominated by seven splendid genealogical figures of the late twelfth century. In the centre is one of the masterpieces of early Gothic glass: a figure of Adam delving after expulsion from Paradise, mattock in hand and clad only in a fleece. On his left are Esron, Naason, Semei; and on his right Joseph, Aminadab and Aram; all these are shown full face with their names in Gothic script behind their heads. They are usually represented as seated on a chair or throne wearing a mantle loosely draped over their tunic; the whole against a background of deep blue.

## The South-West Transept

The greatest display of twelfth-century glass in England is in the large south window of the south-west transept where the vesturer, William Burgys, and his staff placed some twenty-four patriarchal figures from the genealogical series in the choir clerestory in 1792, removing the figures from the centre of each window but leaving

*Lamech (left) and Methusaleh (right) from the south window in the south-west transcept.*

*The funeral of the nurse Britonis from the story of Sir Jordan Fitzeisulf in the Trinity Chapel.*

behind, usually, the borders and armature which enabled
reconstructions of the scheme to be made with good copies from the
originals in the nineteenth century. These twelfth-century figures
reading from left to right are as follows: on the bottom row, Lamech,
Noe, Thare (Terah), Iareth (Jared), Matusale (Methusaleh), Phalech,
Regau and Enoch. Like the ones already described in the west window
of the nave, all are seated against a deep blue ground. Methusaleh is a
venerable figure whose immense age is suggested by the way he leans
his chin on his hand as if too feeble to hold it up unsupported while
Enoch, 'who walked with God', is being gripped by the Divine Hand
which comes out of the clouds above. In the row above are Abraham,
Salmon, Ezechias with the dial of Ahaz in his hand, David with harp,
an unidentified patriarch, Josiah with the scroll of the Law, Boaz
(presumed), and Zorobabel. In the uppermost row of the main lights
are Joanna, Er, Joseph with sceptre, David, Nathan holding a sceptre
topped with a dove, Jonan, Jose and Judah.

The spaces above and below the genealogical figures in each row
are filled up with fragments of ancient glass made up into brilliant
mosaic-like panels. Many coats of arms, either of royal or noble

*Four scenes from the story of William of Gloucester on the south side of the Trinity Chapel.*

families are interspersed. These have been brought from other parts of the church and arranged here with considerable skill. No doubt when this window was glazed in the early years of the fifteenth century there were figures of saints standing in niches intended to simulate the statues around the west front of the cathedral. After the destruction of the three great windows in the western arm of the church by Puritans, nothing remained in the main lights of this window save the pinnacle work which is still in place. In the elaborate tracery at the top of this window can be seen figures of saints and censing angels together with coats of arms of Christ Church Priory, the See of Canterbury and St Thomas, all fifteenth-century work.

Before leaving this transept it is convenient to look at two windows of modern workmanship. That on the west side is by Christopher Whall, sometimes called the last of the pre-Raphaelites. This was inserted in 1903 and in each tier of lights is a scene (unfortunately broken up by the mullions), the lowest being a charming Nativity of Christ, above that the Agony in the Garden, and at the top the Resurrection. Attendant figures act as supporters on each side of the main scenes.

## The Warriors' Chapel

Opposite, in the east window of the Warriors' Chapel of St Michael, the Regimental chapel of the Buffs (the East Kent Regiment), is fine glass of 1952 which replaces a window of mid-nineteenth century glass, a Crimean War Memorial destroyed during the Second World War. This window was the work of William Wilson of Edinburgh and is entirely heraldic. The coats of arms are those of the colonels of the regiment from 1665 to 1957 together with those of royal personages, associated with the regiment, and the arms of the cities of London and Canterbury.

Going up the choir, by way of the gate in the pulpitum screen, we can get some idea of the effect produced by the great band of genealogical figures until the eighteenth-century rearrangement if we look up at the two windows in the clerestory of the eastern transepts adjacent to the ambulatory. Here, on each side, are four figures of the twelfth century, which were not moved, and now, cleaned and restored, these give us some idea of what the glass must have looked like to the monks who worshipped here for more than three hundred and fifty years. The figures on the north side are Shem and Isaac together with two unidentified patriarchs; while on the south side are Neri and Rhesa, Judah and Phares.

## The North-East Transept

In the north wall of the north-east transept is a large circular window, usually decribed as an 'oculus' or early form of those rose windows which are so prominent a feature of the larger French churches and cathedrals from the twelfth to the sixteenth century. This window contains quite a lot of twelfth-century glass, depicting the Old Covenant. A haloed Moses is in the centre holding the Law in the form of a jewelled book; with him is the Synagogue represented by a woman, with head veiled, holding the stone Tables of the Law in her hands. The four Cardinal Virtues are represented in four triangular panels which form a square around this centre panel. All are crowned and their names are on a label: Prudence, Justice, Temperance and Fortitude. Four semi-circular compartments contain the four major prophets, Isaiah, Jeremiah, Ezekiel and Daniel. In the outer part of the window are modern figures of the Minor Prophets to replace those which were probably here originally since the window retains its twelfth-century armatures which bisect into twelve compartments. In the gable opposite, in the south-east

OPPOSITE: *The sower sowing his seed in the north choir ambulatory.*

transept, is a similar rose window which would have had parallel figures of the New Covenant. Apart from some foliage in the background, which may be twelfth-century, what can now be seen is a modern reconstruction of the original scheme: Christ and the Church in the centre surrounded by the Christian Virtues of Faith, Hope, Charity and Humility with the four Evangelistic symbols and twelve apostles.

### The Bible Windows

Two of the most lovely windows in the cathedral are the two Bible Windows in the ambulatory on the north side of the choir. Sometime in the early part of the fourteenth century a monastic scribe recorded the subjects in all the twelve Bible Windows, the types and anti-types as they are usually called, on a parchment roll which is still preserved in the cathedral library, so that it is possible to reconstruct what was in those windows which have lost their glass. The first one to the west has been blocked in and the glass lost. It showed, in the centre medallions, the Annunciation, the Visitation, the Nativity and the appearance of the Angel to the shepherds. The greater part of the second window, walking east, contains the original glass of twenty-one panels arranged in seven tiers of three. From left to right and from top to bottom these are as follows: *(i)* Balaam and his ass; *(ii)* the Magi following the star on splendid horses; *(iii)* Isaiah prophesying at the gate of Jerusalem; *(iv)* Pharoah watching Moses and the Israelites about to cross the Red Sea; *(v)* Herod conversing with the Magi, with the star overhead; *(vi)* Christ converting the heathen from idolatory to the true Faith; *(vii)* Solomon and the Queen of Sheba, whose attendants are accompanied by camels; *(viii)* the Adoration of the Magi and shepherds at Bethlehem; *(xi)* Joseph and his brethren in Egypt with Egyptians in attendance; *(x)* Lot flees from the Cities of the Plain, his wife becoming a pillar of salt; *(xi)* the Magi, suitably crowned, fast asleep in one bed while an angel hovers overhead; *(xii)* Jereboam sacrificing, is rebuked by a prophet for sacrilege; *(xiii)* Samuel is presented to Eli in the tabernacle; *(xiv)* Jesus is presented by His parents in the Temple of Simeon.

From here the original panels which filled the rest of the window, including the Flight into Egypt and the Massacre of the Innocents, have been lost, and their places filled with medallions which have survived from other Bible Windows. On the right of the Presentation scene, where once was a panel showing Melchizideck, the Priest King, offering bread and wine to Abraham, is now a medallion showing the Sower flinging his seed on stony ground with the birds of the air hovering above *(xv)*. In the bottom two rows are the following

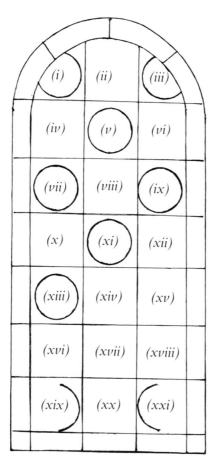

*The second of the Bible windows.*

panels: *(xvi)* Ecclesia, the Church, and the three sons of Noah, Shem, Ham and Japhet dividing the round world between them; *(xvii)* the Pharisees turning away from Jesus (St John 6 v. 66); *(xviii)* three figures representing Virginity, Continence and Marriage, the three blameless states of life in medieval thought; *(xix)* the rich men of the world represented by two Roman Emperors, Julian the Apostate and Maurice; *(xx)* the Sower sowing an abundant crop; and finally *(xxi)* the three righteous men of Old Testament times, Daniel, Job and Noah, who are the seed sown on good ground.

The next window to the east, though apparently complete, is composed of the remains of two windows; this one and the fourth in

the series, which was once in the adjoining transept. At the top a medallion depicts Jesus as a child in the Temple among the doctors; while, in half circles below are Moses and Jethro on the left and Daniel judging the Elders (from the story of Susanna) on the right. In the next medallion is the Marriage at Cana of Galilee with six waterpots prominent in the foreground. Below on the left are the six ages of the world, represented by six Old Testament characters: Adam with hoe, Noah with ark, Abraham with fire and knife, David with crown and harp, Jechonias with crown and sceptre and the Lord Jesus with an open Book of the Gospels. In the half circle on the right are the six Ages of Man from infancy to senility (note the boy with ball and hockey stick).

The third medallion shows the miraculous draught of fishes. The half circle to the left shows Noah looking out of the ark (linked originally with a lost panel of the Baptism of Christ). On the right St Peter, preaching to the Jews, represents the gathering of fish, while two Pharisees, walking away, symbolize the breaking of the net. The fourth medallion shows Nathaniel's call. He sits under the fig tree with Philip. Christ with his apostles, Peter and Andrew, is on the left of the scene. Below in quarter medallions are on the left Gentile hearers and on the right Jewish Pharisees despising the word of God.

Immediately above these Bible Windows, in a little gallery or triforium, are three small windows containing glass which was originally in a similar position further east, looking down into the choir on to the shrines of St Alphege and St Dunstan. These were set at right angles to the High Altar before the Reformation. The two windows to the west contain three scenes each illustrating the story of St Dunstan. In the middle window these are: the vision of St Dunstan invited by angels to spend Ascension Day in heaven (he refused as he wished to minister to his flock on earth that day); to the left, Dunstan, while still a monk at Glastonbury climbing up a ladder and through the roof with the help of an angel, after being shut out of church by the devil and to the right, St Dunstan at Calne, saved miraculously when a floor gave way during a confrontation with dissident clergy who were the unfortunate victims of this accident. In the window to the west of this one are three more scenes from the story of St Dunstan: St Dunstan intercedes for the soul of King Edwy, who is being carried off into the jaws of hell by demons; a roundel of the ordination of Dunstan by Archbishop Odo; and Dunstan, the great

OPPOSITE: *A sainted archbishop from the Water Tower, dating from the fifteenth century.*

*A thirteenth-century panel showing Christ glorified amid symbols of the four Evangelists in a Corona window.*

monastic reformer, separates secular clerks from monks.

The most easterly window in this little gallery is devoted to the monk Archbishop St Alphege, who was martyred by the Danes in 1012 AD. At the top is the siege of Canterbury by the Danes who are strongly resisted by the Saxon citizens. Below the Danes capture the city by treachery and murder both inhabitants and monks despite the intercession of St Alphege. In the right hand roundel the Archbishop is carried off to Margate, where the Danish fleet had anchored, and is forced on board to be taken to the camp at Greenwich to await ransom. Another window, presumably showing the martyrdom at Greenwich, has been lost.

Of the windows over the altars of St Martin and St Stephen, in the north-west transept, illustrating scenes from the lives of those saints only one much restored medallion remains. This shows the famous story of St Martin dividing his cloak with the beggar at Amiens. Restoration or invention of scenes from the lives of both these saints have been attempted in modern times.

*The spies returning with grapes from Canaan from the Corona.*

## The Water Tower

A door in this transept leads to the upper storey of the Norman Water Tower where there is a mixed collection of stained glass. Apostles of the thirteenth century, heraldry and sainted archbishops of the fifteenth century can be seen over the iron railing which normally prevents closer access to the area. A large window on the left side of the tower shows a thirteenth-century scene of the Risen Christ with St Mary Magdalene in the garden after the Resurrection. This was made up of pieces of early thirteenth century glass by Samuel Caldwell about sixty years ago from glass originally in other parts of the cathedral. Some Tudor shields appear in the passage leading to the water tower and that which leads off to the library.

## The Corona

Before inspecting the several windows in the Trinity Chapel we will first look at the centre window of the Corona Chapel. A typological window of the early thirteenth century, it seems to have been an addition to the twelve Bible Windows to which we have already referred and is often known as the Redemption Window. It consists of five panels beginning at the foot with the Crucifixion; above comes the Entombment; then the Resurrection and the Ascension with God in Majesty at the very summit. He is pouring down the Holy Spirit on the figures of the Apostles in a Pentecost scene which is, in fact, the fifth panel. Round each of these New Testament scenes is a little group of Old Testament types. Round the Crucifixion are Moses striking the rock; the Sacrifice of Isaac; the slaughtering of the Passover Lamb; and the spies returning from Canaan with the Grapes of Eshcol. Round the Entombment are Joseph in the Pit; Samson and Delilah in bed, and armed Philistines looking through the door; Jonah thrown overboard and swallowed by the whale; and Daniel in the lions' den in Babylon. Round the Resurrection panel are Noah in the Ark (modern); Jonah vomited from the whale on to the land; David escaping from Saul with the aid of Michal (modern); and Moses and the Burning Bush. Round the Ascension Panel we see the High Priest enter the Holy of Holies; the Assumption of Elijah in a chariot of fire; the sundial of Ahaz and Isaiah standing by the sick bed of Hezekiah; and Enoch taken up to heaven. On the left of the Pentecost panel is the consecration of Aaron and his sons to the priesthood; on the right Moses judges the people of Israel in the presence of Jethro. Below the panel, Moses receives the Tables of the Law from God on Sinai. The background of scrollwork and foliage make this a particularly lovely window. Here, as elsewhere in this early Gothic glass, a notable feature is the fondness of the artists for living creatures such as camels, horses, sheep, and fish as well as birds which appear both in the Bible and the Miracle Windows.

A feature of the methods of glazing used in this period, not always noticed by writers, is the fixing of the leaded panels of glass to iron frames which are then fastened to the permanent ironwork by wedges. When the wedges are removed the panels can be lifted out quickly, as was done immediately after the declaration of war in 1939. On the left of the Redemption window is a large Jesse window, the creation of George Austin in 1861. To the left of this Victorian composition, in a window of plain glass, are the panels of a late twelfth-century Jesse tree. King Josiah and the Blessed Virgin Mary are all that remain of a large window the rest of which has been lost. These panels were bought back for the cathedral in 1953, having been alienated in the nineteenth century.

On the right of the Redemption Window is a late Victorian window illustrating scenes from the Acts of the Apostles, the work of Hemming in 1897. Next to this, set in plain glass is a striking panel of thirteenth-century glass, in a rich border, showing Christ in a mandorla or glory blessing with the symbols of the four Evangelists round him. This was acquired for the cathedral in 1938 and is thought to have come from Petham Church near Canterbury.

*The figure of Jesse from the Corona window (1861).*

## The Trinity Chapel

The most interesting glass, all dating from the early thirteenth century, is that in the Trinity Chapel, where eight windows out of the original twelve still have their medieval armatures. Though much restoration has taken place over the last century the general effect in this beautiful chapel is still enchanting, for the subject is the series of miracles of healing wrought by St Thomas of Canterbury in response to the prayers of devout suppliants. These miracles come from a record compiled on the spot by two of the monks, William and Benedict, at the tomb in the crypt.

The windows begin at the top of the steps and should be read around the north aisle and then round the south aisle of the chapel. The panels and medallions should be examined from the top to the bottom of each window. The first is largely a composition by Samuel Caldwell but with its original borders and several medallions showing scenes from a miracle wrought by the saint on behalf of a man involved in a judicial combat. At the foot of the window is a sainted archbishop, seated on a throne, who is usually identified as St Thomas

*The figure of St Thomas from the north side of the Trinity Chapel.*

himself. It is certainly made up of glass of the twelfth or early thirteenth century and might even be a portrait of St Thomas by someone who remembered him from the time of the murder. The rest of the window, though convincingly early Gothic in feeling, is of modern composition. The second window is a modern one by Clayton and Bell, in a thirteenth-century style, but rather out of place among its famous neighbours.

The next window is set over the entrance to the Chantry of Henry IV. There are three panels of fifteenth-century glass in the chantry windows showing St Christopher, St Edward the Confessor and St Katherine of Alexandria. The two windows above must have been originally of full length to match those on the opposite side of the Trinity Chapel but cut down to allow the insertion of the chantry in

*Trial by combat from the north side of the Trinity Chapel.*

the first half of the fifteenth century. The third window contains ten
miracle scenes. At the top Baldric falls off his horse and is cured by St
Thomas. Then comes the story of Stephen of Hoylake who was
tormented by demons in his dreams and delivered, by prayer, to St
Thomas. The bottom three panels show William the priest of London
delivered from toothache by the touch of the cloak of St Thomas; and
his cure from paralysis by a visit to the tomb in the crypt where a monk
puts a drop of the blood of the martyr in a cup. (A familiar aspect of
the tomb, which occurs again and again in these windows, is a lectern
with a book on it and a money box, usually green in colour, lying on
the tomb for offerings, often with a monk in attendance.)

In the fourth window are pairs of roundels in eight tiers set in a
deep blue border with a diaper of foliage and berries. Some of the
panels in these windows are modern insertions intended to give a
sense of completeness and certainly better than leaving gaps filled
only with plain glass. Among the most interesting of the miracles
recorded here are *(iii)* and *(iv)* showing Petronilla of Polesworth, an
epileptic nun, who has a fit in the presence of her abbess and is taken
to the tomb in the crypt where her feet are bathed in holy water, after

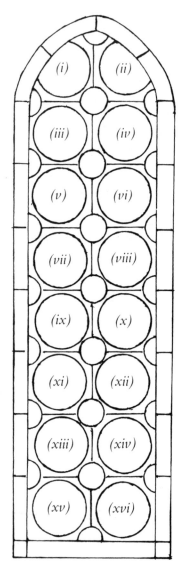

*The fourth window of the Trinity Chapel.*

which she begins to recover. In *(viii)* King Louis VII of France dreams that St Thomas has appeared to inform him that his son and heir, who is very ill, will recover and that, in return for the efficacious prayers of the saint, the King must make a pilgrimage to the tomb at Canterbury.

*Henry of Fordwich at the tomb of St Thomas.*

(This is a historical incident and Louis in 1179 did make the pilgrimage of thanksgiving; it is recorded that he gave the monks a vineyard at Poissy, near Paris, also a great ruby called the Regale of France which was subsequently placed on the Shrine in the Trinity Chapel.) *(ix)* and *(x)* tell the story of Robert of Cricklade, Prior of the Austin Canons of St Frideswide at Oxford. He is seen bathing his swollen feet in holy water at the tomb and then, cured, casting aside his cloak and boots.

In *(xiii)* and *(xiv)* Henry of Fordwich, a maniac, is brought by his keepers to the tomb; they are armed with cudgels and cords, which are shown as cast away beside the tomb where he kneels at prayer, after his restoration to sanity. (In each of the scenes, in which cures or answers to prayers to the saint are depicted, the simple message to the pilgrim is that St Thomas' prayers are of great power before God, that a pilgrimage to Canterbury is the proper way to show gratitude and a thankoffering is something the saint has a right to expect.)

The fifth window is, in some respects the most interesting of the series, and the most reminiscent of contemporary glass in Chartres, Sens or Rouen. This is partly due to the fact that the four large roundels, which constitute the main design of the window, are set in a

*A knight on horseback returning from pilgrimage.*

gorgeous background of blue glass with a rectangular diaper with small ruby flowers at the intersections, and there is a good deal of scroll work with much green and ruby glass all through the window. At the top of the window, in the first roundel, is a famous representation of the golden shrine set up here in 1220. The martyr is seen emerging from the shrine in a vision to one of the monks, who appears to be sleeping in a bed in the shrine area. This may even be Benedict or his colleague William who spent so much time noting down details of the cures at the tomb. The second roundel is filled with modern glass.

In the third large roundel is set out the story of Eilward of Westoning, a story of rough medieval justice. Eilward is brought before a magistrate accused of stealing property from his neighbour, Fulk. He is sentenced to blinding and mutilation and the magistrate supervises the carrying out of this savage sentence. In a small inset below Thomas appears in a vision to the poor wretch as he lies in bed and signs him with the sign of the Cross. Eilward, his sight wondrously restored, displays his eyes to a band of pilgrims who bestow on him alms, which he promptly gives away to a beggar. In another small inset he gives thanks at the tomb. At the top of this roundel a man, perhaps a knight, rides out of a gateway from a city: this does not seem to have any connection with the story of Eilward. At the foot of the window in the bottom roundel is the story of a sick monk, Hugh the Cellarer of Melrose Abbey, who is seen receiving extreme unction from his abbot. He is given water from the well of St Thomas in the crypt to drink, blood pours from his nose and he is thereupon cured. The usual panel, showing him as a pilgrim at the tomb, has been lost and replaced by a modern copy.

The sixth window is very large and the most enjoyable of all the series in the stories of miracles that it tells. It has thirty-three scenes, some being replacements of lost glass, all arranged in a complicated pattern of interlocking circles with square panels interposed.

The top three panels tell the story of Juliana of Rochester who is cured of blindness after a visit to the tomb. Very enjoyable because of the prominence of horses in the story is that of Richard Sunieve of Edgeworth which fills the six panels below. He was a farm labourer who drove his master's horses to the fields, fell asleep apparently healthy and awoke to find himself a leper. He goes to Canterbury, is cured and then goes back with his mother, master and mistress to offer a gift of money at the tomb.

Then comes a cautionary tale about another Rochester character, Robertulus (little Bobby), whose pleasure it was to wander down to the River Medway and stone the frogs. He fell in one day and was apparently drowned. His playmates reported the matter to his parents who are seen weeping as they fish the body out at low tide (the inevitable sequel of the successful intervention of St Thomas in response to the agonized prayers of the parents and the pilgrimage to Canterbury is lost). Another story tells of a maniac cured, in this case Matilda of Cologne who is brought to Canterbury after murdering her baby and is seen in a state of collapse at the tomb. Then, having been cured, she gives thanks while her keepers, no doubt relieved at the prospect of a more agreeable journey home, stand by with cudgels at rest.

Perhaps the most enjoyable story in the whole series fills nine panels at the bottom of the window. These depict the trials and tribulations which befell Sir Jordan Fitzeisulf, a friend of St Thomas, who constantly delayed to fulfil a pledge to make a pilgrimage to the tomb of the saint. The series begins on the bottom left with the funeral of Britonis, the old nurse of the family. This is a wonderful picture of a country funeral in the early thirteenth century with the coffin, covered in a golden pall, carried by four men while the parish priest,

*ABOVE:* Pilgrims bringing holy water to the sick child, from the story of Sir Jordan Fitzeisulf.

*BELOW:* St Thomas threatens Sir Jordan Fitzeisulf's family with the plague.

*Two scenes showing pilgrims offering gifts at the shrine of St Thomas from the Miracle Windows.*

in alb, goes in front sprinkling holy water. The son of the house, William, is dying while his stricken parents look on and the priest sprinkles him with holy water. Pilgrims from Canterbury bring holy water from the well in the crypt which Sir Jordan pours down his son's throat. Above, Sir Jordan, grateful for the child's recovery, promises a thankoffering of coins at St Thomas' tomb in mid-Lent. The boy, recovered, sits up in bed eating food while his parents look thankfully on. But the promised offering in Canterbury is not made. St Thomas appears in a dream to a poor leper, Gimp, to tell him to warn Sir Jordan the penalties he will incur if he continues to put off the promised pilgrimage. Gimp, from his sickbed conveys the warning but it is ignored. The eldest son dies, several servants fall ill as well as Sir Jordan and his wife. (In this dramatic scene St Thomas is seen hovering above the stricken household with a drawn sword in his hand.) At last the pilgrimage takes place. The family, with a bowl of coins are seen approaching the tomb.

On the other side of the chapel the windows in the south ambulatory have suffered much more than those already inspected. These were protected by various medieval buildings connected with the monastic infirmary which were still in use down to the latter part of the nineteenth century when they were demolished. No such buildings masked the Trinity Chapel on the south side so iconoclasts and vandals, armed with muskets, stones and other weapons of destruction, seemed to have had every opportunity of 'rattling down Becket's miraculous deeds' here.

*Adam the Forester shot by a poacher from the south side of the Trinity Chapel.*

The first window nearest the Corona is full of old glass, but the upper eight medallions were made up, in 1893, from fragments though the borders and background seem to be original. The bottom eight medallions are worth attention as they tell the stories of two men miraculously healed. William of Kellet, the 'unskilful carpenter' cuts his leg with an axe while at work. In a dream St Thomas appears to him and restores his leg to normal. A woman, who comes to attend to his leg, finds no sign of the wound when she unlooses the bandage. William is shown returning from the pilgrimage. Exultant at his recovery, he holds an axe in his hand and has two fastened in his belt. The city gate is behind him and a tree, suggesting a forest, is on the right.

Then comes the story of Adam the forester who, encountering poachers, is shot by one through the throat while another carries off a deer on his back. Adam drinks the holy water of St Thomas and is visited by friends. Recovered from his wound, Adam makes his thankoffering at the tomb. This story recalls the adventures of Robin Hood, who traditionally flourished in the reign of King John, when these windows were made.

The eighth window is filled with plain glass as is the tenth. The window between them has plain glass relieved by two panels of the

*Pilgrims on their way to Canterbury from the south side of the Trinity Chapel.*

early thirteenth century and border work of the same period. These were placed here about 1929. One of the panels shows pilgrims on the road to Canterbury, one riding on a white horse. He is bearded and followed by a young man, a woman and a third man who walks with a crutch or staff as a cripple might. The other panel shows pilgrims at the tomb over which hangs a sanctuary lamp with a priest in attendance. The eleventh window contains much glass gathered from various parts of the cathedral by Samuel Caldwell in the first quarter of the present century. The top panels tell the story of John of Roxburgh, a groom, whose horse bolted and threw him into the River Tweed. He was rescued by the intercession of St Thomas, and is shown creeping from the river to a toll house by a bridge where, placed by a roaring fire, he is restored 'in his whole body'. Among the interesting scenes shown in this window are two half medallions which tell the story of Gilbert, the young son of William le Brun who, after being given up for dead is shown in a state of recovery, sitting up in bed, to the delight of his parents. They make a pilgrimage to the tomb where the boy makes an offering of a coil of wire.

Next is another large window with twenty-two scenes, which has two pictures at the bottom, showing the shrine which makes it clear that they were designed at the end of 1220 or soon after. Here again the offering of a coil of wire suggests that this was some kind of accepted votive offering at this point in the history of pilgrimages. The altar, which stood at the west end of the shrine, appears in each scene. Immediately above these are eight panels which tell the story of William of Gloucester. He was a workman in the service of Becket's old enemy, Archbishop Roger de Pont L'Evêque of York, who was building a palace for his master at Churchdown in Gloucestershire when a mound of earth collapsed on him as he was laying drainpipes. The panels depict his rescue by the villagers, organized by the parish priest. One must presume he prayed to St Thomas while the villagers dug the unfortunate William out. Since he was found to be alive much credit went to St Thomas and no doubt the story ended with the usual pilgrimage and offering. A similar story is depicted at the top of the window. A child, Geoffrey of Winchester, is saved by St Thomas from death by fever. He nearly perishes, later, when a gale brings down a wall on top of his cradle. The mother faints at the spectacle but revives sufficiently to invoke St Thomas. In due course when the servants have cleared the ruins the child is discovered unhurt.

To the right above this tale is a very interesting example of medical practice in the early thirteenth century. A sick monk, who may be a leper, is seated on the left of the panel. His abbot, holding his crosier, is on the right. Two men appear to be examining a phial which they hold up to the light. It has been suggested that these are physicians making an uroscopic examination. This deep blue window, which has been recently cleaned and restored is one of the most brilliant in the series, composed of panels arranged in fan-shaped pairs within a rich border.

## St Anselm's Chapel

Descending the Pilgrims' Steps on the south side, the next window to catch the eye of the glass lover is that in St Anselm's Chapel. This is a large, five-light window, the stone work dating from 1336 when it was installed in 1959, the work of the distinguished glazier, Harry Archbishop Simon Meopham. No record of the glass, which was originally designed for this window has survived, but the present glass was installed in 1959, the work of the distinguised glazier, Harry Stammers of York. It has five figures in the main lights with St Anselm, full face in the centre with his most famous book, 'Cur Deus Homo', shown below. On his left are King William Rufus and Anselm's patron, Lanfranc. On his right stands his friend and physician, the monk Baldwin as well as King Henry I. There are small scenes under each figure, in which these characters played some part in the life of the sainted Archbishop. In the stone tracery is a rose in which a Paschal Lamb is depicted. Altogether this makes a very rich and impressive window with much white glass contrasted with reds, golds and some strong green.

## The South-East Transept

In the south-east transept are four windows of the same period as the Stammers Window, the work of the Hungarian refugee artist, Ervin Bossanyi. He designed and made these to replace glass destroyed in June 1942. They were all worked in the decade between 1950 and 1960, the first to be placed in position in 1956 being the right hand window in the south wall called Peace. Christ, as the Ancient of Days, stands with children at his feet enjoying the blessings of peace poured forth by an angel. The window on the left of this one, called Salvation, was inserted in 1958. In this a man is shown being delivered from captivity by an angel to be reunited with his son and daughter, while others beneath await salvation. A cross, glowing at the summit, reminds us that salvation comes from Christ alone. In the wall above are two smaller windows. The left hand one shows Peter walking on the water to Christ. That on the right is a representation of St Christopher, the 'gentle giant' of legend, carrying the Christ Child on his back. St Christopher is an appropriate saint to find here since he has continued to be the patron saint of travellers in modern times as he was in the Middle Ages.

Two Victorian windows of good quality by George Austin (1852) survived the assaults of war and appear over the altar of St John the Evangelist and St Gregory respectively. The first is a Jesse Tree, a smaller version of the large one in the Corona, while the second has, among other roundels, copies of two panels, which were at some time alienated from the cathedral and are now in the Virginia Museum of Fine Arts, USA.

## The South Choir Ambulatory

In the little gallery or lower triforium of the south choir ambulatory are three windows of thirteenth-century glass, very much restored and brought from other parts of the cathedral. The first window from the east shows scenes from the apocryphal life of the Blessed Virgin Mary: she falls asleep in the presence of the Apostles; she is carried up into heaven by angels; and her Divine Son crowns her amid censing angels. The next window shows the Crucifixion, the Resurrection, and the Ascension of Christ. The third window, which seems to have come originally from the clerestory of the apse, has three panels: the Nativity with Mary and Joseph with the Child, the ox and ass, and a shepherd worshipping; the Adoration of the Magi; and the Presentation of Christ in the Temple.

The large windows below, three in number, included originally a final pair of the 'Bible Windows' but it seems probable that the glass was all smashed by the Puritans in 1642. The Victorian glass placed here in the last part of the nineteenth century was destroyed in the raid of 1 June 1942. Some pieces of thirteenth-century French glass, acquired by the agents of the American newspaper magnate William Randolph Hearst were put up for sale, after his death and bought by representatives of the Dean and Chapter. Between 1958 and 1962 these were set here in modern glass surrounds in thirteenth-century style by George Easton, who had worked for many years as assistant to Samuel Caldwell. In the most easterly window of the three, roundels show scenes from the apocryphal life of St Andrew the Apostle: the Saint riding round his diocese of Patras on a white horse; his arrest by armed men; and then stripped for execution he is laid 'saltire-wise' on a tree cross. The middle window is composed of a number of disconnected scenes. Ten in all, they include the conversion of St Paul on the Damascus road, the martyrdom of a bishop by armed men with swords, possibly that of St Thomas Becket, as well as the Annunciation. The third window has three large roundels and some smaller pieces of old glass. The roundels include the flight of the Holy Family in to Egypt; the legendary attempt to boil St John the Divine in oil before the Latin Gate at Rome; and a Doom or Last Judgement with demons carrying off the souls of the damned to hell.

## The Crypt

From this point one can descend into the crypt for a brief visit to see a few pieces of ancient glass. The east window in the apsidal Jesus Chapel contains its original border and a very attractive panel of thirteenth-century glass showing the Virgin and Child with censing angels. This came from St Alban's court at Nonington, near Canterbury, when the house and its contents were sold in 1938. It probably was originally in the cathedral, which seems to have lost a lot of old glass at different times, notably in the Victorian era. Contemporary glass figures of Isaiah, Jeremiah, Jacob and Isaac, like those in the Water Tower fill the space below this panel. Underneath is a scene which appears to come from one of the Miracle Windows, as yet unidentified. A much restored panel at the foot of the window shows the Crucifixion. In the windows of the apsidal chapels of St Mary Magdalene and St Nicholas are scenes showing St Mary Magdalene anointing the feet of Christ and four little scenes from the legend of St Nicholas, the Bishop of Myra. Miscellaneous pieces,

*The decorated border of the Jesse window of 1861 in the Corona.*

mostly of late medieval date, appear in the windows of St Gabriel's Chapel and the aisle outside. In 1984 a small diamond shaped panel, executed by Frederick Cole, to the memory of George Easton (the chapter glazier whose life was given to the care of ancient glass), was inserted in a window in the western crypt as a tribute from the Worshipful Company of Glaziers and Painters of Glass.

### The North-West Transept

Leaving the dim, religious light of the Romanesque crypt and climbing the old Norman staircase into the bright light of the north-west transept one finds oneself in the fifteenth century with much glass of the period as an epilogue to the tour of the windows. The huge window in the north wall must have been one of the most magnificent in England when it was first inserted, and is usually known as the Royal Window since it was the gift of Edward IV to commemorate the marriage of his ancestor Edward I, to Margaret of France in this same transept in 1299. It is thought to have been ordered by the King when he paid one of his many visits to Canterbury in 1465. The glass in the main lights of the window may have come from the workshop of William Neve, the Royal glazier, who was appointed in 1476 and was at work for the next decade. The tracery glass is still intact but the most impressive feature still to be seen are portraits of the whole Royal family of England, 1480, with coats of arms above their heads in the main lights. The great figures of St Thomas and our Lady's seven glorious appearances as well as St George, the Blessed Trinity and the twelve Apostles were deliberately destroyed on 13 December 1643.

Bernard Rackham has pointed out the strong differences in style between the tracery and the royal figures in the middle of the window. We may conclude that the numerous figures in the tracery lights were inserted some years before the main lights of the window were glazed. He describes the tracery figures as 'low in tone and linear in drawing while the royal figures and the heraldic angels are executed in glass of a strong colour with heavy shading'. At the top of the window are the coats of Edward IV and Cardinal Archbishop Thomas Bourchier with eight prophets in the row below and twelve apostles underneath them. More interesting than these conventional figures are fourteen saints in the bottom row of the tracery, most of whom have some special connection with Canterbury. From left to right these are Saints Denis, Wilfred, Augustine of Hippo, Martin, Jerome, Dunstan, Thomas Becket, Augustine of Canterbury, Anselm, Nicolas, Blasius, Alphege and Ouen. There are seven main lights to the window with angels holding coats of arms at the top and, below, more angels holding royal coats.

The royal portrait gallery begins on the left with Richard, Duke of York, behind whose kneeling figure is a tapestry embroidered with his device, the falcon and the fetterlock. Next to him kneels his brother, Edward, Prince of Wales, who though never crowned is usually known as Edward V, with the ostrich feathers and motto 'Ich dien' behind him. These tragic young princes both wear coronets. Their father King Edward IV kneels in the third light, crowned and robed very magnificently with a sceptre in his gloved hand. On his predieu is a figure of St George and the Dragon, and on the ruby tapestry his badge, the Sun in Splendour. The coat of arms in the centre light, probably that of Henry VII, was inserted much later, perhaps in place of a crucifix which would have been the natural centrepiece of a window in which all the characters face inwards. The crucifix may have been smashed in the debacle of 1643. Queen Elizabeth Woodville kneels facing her husband, crowned and reading a prayer book, against a blue tapestry embroidered with columbines, her particular device. Behind her, in the two remaining lights, are five daughters of the marriage headed by Elizabeth, the White Rose of York, whose marriage to Henry VII ended the Wars of the Roses. Her sisters Cecily, Anne, Katherine and Mary kneel behind her, the death of the last, in 1482, providing a 'terminus ad quem' to the making of the window.

## The Chapel of Our Lady Martyrdom

Leading out of the transept is the lovely fifteenth-century Chapel of Our Lady Martyrdom. In its east window are five richly coloured coats of arms connected with Archbishop Bourchier, set in a cool background of quarries painted with various badges of his family. These include falcons, the slipped knot, which was the Bourchier badge, and stems of oak leaves.

Leaving the transept by the cloister door, we pass beneath a window whose glass is the work of the studio of Sir Ninian Comper. This was inserted in 1954, a gift of the Freemasons of Kent. It is somewhat overcrowded with portraits of royal and other personalities who had some part in the Coronation of Queen Elizabeth II, and also that of her father George VI. Its best feature is an Annunciation in the tracery and below this three coats of arms which have survived from medieval times. John Barnewell, a London merchant, who gave the original glass in memory of his father, Thomas, 1446 supplied the priory with fish and wine which explains the arms: those of the City of London, the Saltfishmongers Company and the Barnewell family.

In the cloisters the tracery lights of two bays in the west wall contain charming glass by Hugh Easton. One shows figures connected with Church music: Purcell, Tallis, Merbecke and Archbishop Stephen Langton. The glass in the adjoining window, dedicated in 1946 in memory of Dean 'Dick' Sheppard, depicts the Infant Christ adored by the shepherds, one of whom is a portrait of 'Dick' himself. Supporting figures are those of St Martin, the soldier saint and St Thomas of Canterbury who clasps a broken sword. These and some figures of archbishops by Geoffrey Webb in the east walk are all that have been completed of a scheme planned half a century ago for glazing the whole cloister in this way.

## The Chapter House

The Chapter House is lit by two huge windows in the east and west walls, the work of the firm of Hemming. The east window, given by the Freemasons of Kent in 1896, contains twenty-four figures from the history of the cathedral beginning with Ethelbert, Bertha and Augustine and ending with Victoria (see p. 6). The west window, given in memory of Dean Farrar 1903, has corresponding scenes, in which each of the historical figures played some part. A great deal of heraldry in the traceries of these windows completes an ensemble of colour which makes these windows, not only a pictorial history book, but also, a striking feature of the largest Chapter House in the United Kingdom to have survived from medieval times.

*Chapter Five*

# THE TOMBS AND MONUMENTS OF THE CATHEDRAL

C ANTERBURY'S RICH collection of tombs and monuments from the thirteenth century onwards can best be seen by walking in a long clockwise loop from the north-west tower up the north aisle of the nave, visiting the Martyrdom Transept and then the Trinity Chapel via the north ambulatory of the choir. From there St Anselm's Chapel and the Warriors' Chapel of St Michael in the south-west transept can be visited before descending to the crypt and finally returning down the south aisle of the nave.

### The North Aisle of the Nave

On the west wall of the Chapel of St Augustine, under the north-west tower is a list of the archbishops of Canterbury from Augustine to the present day. The first tomb one sees is that of Edward White Benson, Archbishop from 1883-1897 and the first primate to be buried in his own cathedral since Cardinal Pole in 1558. His monument, designed by T.G. Jackson, with an effigy by Thomas Brock, is an uninspired version of that of his thirteenth-century predecessor John Peckham in the Martyrdom Transept.

Other monuments in the north aisle in the same 'mock Gothic' manner are those of Dean Lyall (1845-1856), Archbishop Sumner (1848-1862), and Edward Parry (Bishop of Dover, 1870-1890), the latter with an effigy of marble by James Forsyth. Just by the north door of the nave is a handsome tablet of 1612 to the memory of Hadrian de Saravia, a prebendary of Flemish extraction who became a zealous Anglican and was one of the translators of the Authorised Version of the Bible. At the far end of the nave is another tablet of the same period to Richard Colfe, vice dean, one of a family who fled

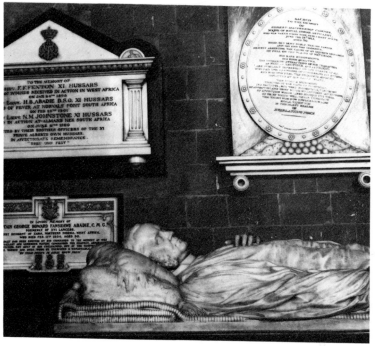

*An effigy of Bishop Parry of Dover in the nave.*

from Calais at the time of its capture in 1558 and settled in Canterbury.

There are two monuments of the late Elizabethan period on this north wall. Sir John Boys, who died in 1602, was recorder of Canterbury and steward to five archbishops and the founder of an almshouse, Jesus Hospital, which is still in use today. He is shown reclining in ruff and legal gown with his two daughters kneeling below on the front of the tomb. A three-decker monument commemorates members of the old Kentish family of Hales. Sir James died at sea during the attack on Cadiz in 1589, in reprisal for the Spanish Armada the previous year, and is shown being dropped overboard from a ship of the line; his widow, Alice, kneels at a prediu below and their son, Chenies, appears at the foot of this hanging monument. A dashing young Elizabethan gallant in appearance, he only survived his father by seven years.

Prominent amongst the pompous mock-medieval creations of the Gothic revival is the charming tablet to the illustrious Jacobean composer, Orlando Gibbons. Appointed organist of Westminster

MEM...... .........

IACOBO HALES, MILITI VIR.....VS ET M.......VS C.VERV.INSIGNI.ET.PATRIÆ CHARO IN
EXPEDITION. PORTVGAL.......A......PATRIAM REVERSVS ANNO.D.1589.OBIIT
D.ALICIÆ EIVSDEM IACOBI........EA FORMOS........MIS MATER.....OS PIETATIS DOTIBVS
ORNATÆ QVÆ ....APRIL.D.1592: MORTVA EST.
CHENEIO HALES VNICO ..R.VNI.EM IACOBI ..ALICIÆ FILIO GEN ANNO:D:1596
IMMATVRO FAT........
.....ARDVS LEE ARMIGER EIVSDEM A...
P..RITVS SVPERSTE..MÆRENS.ON....

Abbey in 1623, he came down to Canterbury in 1625 to superintend the music at the wedding of Charles I to Henrietta Maria but he died suddenly of apoplexy on his way out of morning service in the cathedral on Whitsunday while waiting for the couple to arrive in Canterbury from Dover. He was promptly buried in the nave and his widow, Elizabeth, paid thirty-two pounds to Nicholas Stone for his memorial tablet, the centre piece of which is a fine portrait bust. On the wall, close by, is the hanging organ case designed by Noel Mander and given to the cathedral in 1980 by Lord Astor of Hever, a fitting memorial to his term of office as Seneschal from 1974 to shortly before his death in 1984.

Of some interest are several works by Henry Weekes, a local boy educated at the King's School and the sculptor of the obelisk on the tall mound in the Dane John Gardens of the city. Apart from the tomb of Archbishop Sumner, he was responsible for the bust of Dr Welfitt, prebendary from 1807 to 1854, in this aisle, and also for another bust, in the south aisle, of Sir George Gipps who was Governor-in-Chief of New South Wales when he died in 1847.

A tablet of some distinction by the famous sculptor, John Flaxman, commemorates Thomas Laurence, President of the Royal College of Physicians. Flaxman was paid 80 guineas for this work which was completed in 1805. A marble tablet commemorates Lieutenant Boswell Bennett who was shot dead on 13 May 1838 during the 'Battle of Bossenden Wood' while striving to arrest a mad demagogue, who styled himself 'Sir William Courtenay, Knight of Malta'. Other military heroes with tablets here of some interest are Major Robert Macpherson-Carnes, of the Royal Horse Artillery, killed 'on the plains of Waterloo', 18 June 1815 and that to Colonel Edgar Ravenhill 1907, carved with beautiful lettering by the distinguished artist, Eric Gill.

## The North-West Transept

The north-west transept of the cathedral attracts multitudes all through the year and especially on 29 December for it was here, on that day, that Thomas Becket was martyred, just inside the cloister door. The stone on which his head traditionally lay after the murder, is still preserved in the floor and beside it can be seen an inscribed stone which records the fact that Pope John Paul II and Archbishop Robert Runcie knelt and prayed there together on 29 May 1982. Many indents of brasses of medieval priors and archbishops can be

OPPOSITE: *The Hales Monument in the north nave aisle.*

seen forming the pavement of this transept, the brasses having been torn up all over the cathedral by the iconoclasts in the seventeenth century. Of the many post-Reformation ledger stones and wall tablets, the most interesting person commemorated is Dr John Bargrave, canon from 1662-1680, whose well-worn stone is immediately inside the cloister door. On his travels abroad during Cromwell's Protectorate he collected a kind of private museum of objects of interest which he bequeathed to the cathedral, along with his 'octoangular' dining table. He rounded off his travels in 1662 with a journey to Algiers to ransom Christian slaves captured by the pirates who preyed on shipping from that port in the Mediterranean. 'I bought them slave by slave as one bought horses in Smithfield but it was a thousand to one that I and my fellow commissioner had been made slaves,' he wrote on his safe return, having rescued 127 captives for £10,000.

Two great archiepiscopal tombs fill the north wall of the transept. John Peckham (1279-1294), the only Franciscan to become archbishop, has a handsome tomb under an ogee canopy carved with vine leaves. Nine figures of bishops are carved on the front and five on the sides. His effigy is of oak but the mitre has disappeared. The next tomb is that of William Warham (1503-1533) a friend of Erasmus and Holbein and a Christian humanist. On the tomb is a stone effigy of Warham in full pontificals; the chantry attached to it along the north wall of the transept was demolished and the tomb badly restored in 1796.

## The Chapel of Our Lady and St Benedict

Leading out of the transept is the Chapel of Our Lady and St Benedict, so full of the tombs of post-Reformation deans that until recently it was always known as the Deans' Chapel. Inside the chapel gate on the left is the plain altar tomb of Dean Rogers (1584-1597) who was also Bishop of Dover. It has a Latin epitaph carved on it and some coats of arms. On the wall above is a large Baroque tablet commemorating Dr Thomas Turner who returned with Charles II in 1660 to become dean and preside over the huge and costly restoration of the cathedral after the neglect and depredations of the Puritan regime.

Dr John Boys, who became dean in 1619 has the grandest and most costly monument in this chapel. Robed in cassock, gown and ruff he sits at a table in his library in the deanery with a book open in front of him. He is supposed to have been found in this position after he died. Not long before his death he had preached before Charles I and his Queen, Henrietta Maria when they visited the cathedral after their

*A marble effigy of Archbishop Henry Chichele in life, above, and in death, below.*

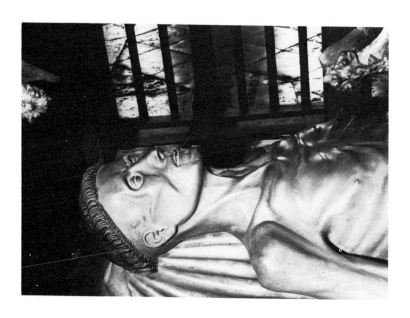

marriage in June 1625. The tomb of Dean Fotherby, his predecessor, is even more gruesome, festooned with skulls and bones and other emblems of mortality. Above his tomb on the wall is a circular portrait on copper of Boys' successor, Dean Isaac Bargrave, 1625-1643, who was chaplain to Charles I and a strong churchman in the Laudian tradition. His portrait was the work of Cornelius Janssen of Utrecht, a friend of the Dean's nephew Dr John Bargrave who commissioned it in 1679. It was at the end of his life that the fanatical Puritans headed by Blue Dick Culmer sacked the cathedral, doing incalculable damage to glass, statues and to all the furniture of the church. The Dean himself was thrown into prison and did not long survive the cruel treatment he and his wife received. Another victim of the religious intolerance of this period, James Wedderburn, lies under a slab in the floor. He was appointed Bishop of Dunblane by the influence of Laud, whose chaplain he had been, but was driven from his Scottish See in 1637, and died in Canterbury where he had fled for refuge in 1639. His friend and pupil, the distinguished scholar Meric Casaubon, who was canon of the cathedral, is buried under a simple slab in the nave.

### The North Choir Ambulatory

At the top of the steps leading from nave to north ambulatory, is a wall tablet to another canon of this period, Alexander Chapman, Archdeacon of Stow and Chaplain to Elizabeth the 'Winter Queen of Bohemia'. This is a fine portrait bust showing him in clerical garb and ruff. It was only moved to this position in 1970 having, for three and a half centuries, looked down from the wall on the place of the murder of St Thomas. A handsome memorial in the north-east transept shows Archbishop Archibald Tate 1868-1883, a great Victorian primate, in rochet and chimere, this effigy being the work of Sir E. Boehm. The tomb-like monument is made up of coloured marbles and carries an inscription composed by Dean Vaughan which reads thus, 'A great archbishop, just, discerning, dignified, statesmanlike; wise to know the time and resolute to redeem it. He had one mission to make the Church of England more and more the Church of the people drawing towards it both by word and example all who love things true and pure, beautiful and of good report'.

In St Martin's Chapel, close to this monument, furnished as a memorial to Lord Alfred Milner are two interesting medieval scratchings on the wall. One reads 'Ediva Regina' and commemorates the Saxon Queen, who was a most generous benefactor to the monks; while the other equally simple reads, 'Lanfranc', in memory of one of the greatest of all archbishops. Under the adjoining altar of St Stephen

*The mosaic pavement and floor of the Trinity Chapel from the Watching Chamber, showing the tomb of Henry IV.*

lie the ashes of Archbishop Cosmo Lang 1928-1942, whose coat of arms, impaled with the Sees of York and Canterbury, is carved on the walls of the chapel. A tablet on the opposite wall is to the memory of Archdeacon Benjamin Harrison, a Tractarian Canon, who presented to the Chapter the splendid Howley-Harrison library, housed in a building of mellow, old brick a few yards away near the Water Tower.

Three interesting archbishops are commemorated on the north side of the presbytery. Henry Chichele 1414-1443, founder of All Souls College, Oxford has, perhaps, the most colourful tomb in the cathedral. This is a double decker which shows him in full pontificals on the top with little clerks kneeling beside him in prayer, and depicted as a ghastly corpse in a shroud below. The tomb was thoroughly restored at the expense of All Souls College in 1897. The statues and heraldry are the work of the well known Victorian artist C.E. Kempe and needed very little attention in 1947 when the college carried out the inspection of the tomb which is traditional every half century. Complete with its distinctive iron railing crested with star flowers and fleur de lys, the tomb was installed in 1425 long before Chichele's death. Next to it is that of William Howley which is the first of a series of monuments of Victorian archbishops in a style which imitates the medieval tombs around the building. The effigy here shows him in a coronation cope and is the work of Richard Westmacott, the younger son of a distinguished sculptor 1799-1872.

Howley was the donor of the great stone throne across the choir and had the distinction of baptizing, confirming, crowning and marrying Queen Victoria. He died, finally, in 1848. The very grand tomb next to this with a tall canopy surmounting a large Gothic arch is that of Cardinal Archbishop Bourchier, a great grandson of Edward III, who was in office from 1452-1486. The tomb itself is probably made lofty so as not to prevent light from the ambulatory windows falling on the High Altar. There is no effigy but a fine brass inscription asking for prayers for the dead man's soul and the dark brown stonework is carved with Bourchier devices: knots and fructed oak leaves. Most of the statues which filled the numerous niches have gone but four little statues of St Katherine of Alexandria have survived, probably having escaped the notice of the usual 'image breakers'. On the wall opposite the tomb is a charming little tablet to Thomas Cockes, a local character who was auditor or clerk to the Chapter and is remembered for his manuscript account book which tells us a good deal about life in the cathedral and its Precincts between 1584 and 1611.

*The canopy of Henry IV's tomb.*

At the top of the Pilgrim Steps, on the north side of the Trinity Chapel lie buried Henry IV and his consort, Queen Joan of Navarre. The tomb of the only King of England to be buried in the cathedral seems oddly placed so near that of the Black Prince, whose son Richard II Henry supplanted and for whose murder he must be held responsible. For all this it is a glorious royal sepulchre with alabaster effigies depicting the royal couple crowned and robed in great splendour. Dr John Harvey suggests that the tomb and effigies may have been the work of Robert Broun, who lived in the Savoy in London between 1414 and 1421. Over the tomb hangs an elaborate wooden tester, richly carved and painted with many shields of arms including much royal heraldry, most likely the work of William Toutmond, chief carpenter to the King. He died in 1415 two years after the King and it seems likely that the tomb itself and some of its appurtenances may have been constructed in Henry IV's lifetime. Notable features of this monument are the paintings on wooden boards of the martyrdom of St Thomas at the west end, and of the Coronation of Our Lady at the other end; an elaborate carved shield with the arms of King and Queen on the exterior of the tomb at the west end; and a handsome iron railing resembling those around the tombs of Chichele, Courtenay and the Black Prince. Since all these railings are interspersed with tall iron posts for candles which would burn on obit days and high feasts, and all have the same decorated motifs of fleur de lys alternating with lions' heads it can be presumed that all were produced at the same time from the same smithy.

In the next bay is the most handsome Renaissance tomb in the cathedral, that of Dr Nicholson Wotton, the first dean of the new foundation 1542-1566. He was a most accomplished diplomat, sent on many missions abroad by the Tudor sovereigns and especially trusted by Henry VIII who made him an executor of his will and left him a legacy. He was a disastrous dean, seldom coming to Canterbury and never to York, a deanery which he held simultaneously with Canterbury. As a result of his absenteeism the twelve prebendaries quarrelled and squandered all the plate and vestments left for the proper performance of divine service under the new regime. His considerable fortune was left to his nephew, Thomas, who set up this tomb which depicts the Dean as a little man with curly hair kneeling at a predieu in full surplice and DD hood, an obelisk towering up behind him. A fulsome inscription in Latin sets out his achievements and preferments, reinforced by coats of arms in bright colours, all protected by a lovely iron railing contemporary with the tomb.

In an embrasure opposite, under one of the Miracle Windows is the cenotaph of Dr Randall Davidson, 1903-1928 who was the first archbishop ever to resign and probably the last to have this kind of mock medieval monument, since his three successors all have chapels in the cathedral furnished in their memory instead. The Australian sculptor, Cecil Thomas, was the artist responsible for the bronze effigy, showing him in a cope giving his blessing, lying on a bed of Hoptonwood stone, decorated on the front with coats of arms of the Sees of which he was bishop.

### The Corona

In the Corona, now dedicated to the saints and martyrs of our own time, are commemorated two archbishops of different eras and

*The Pilgrim Steps and the tombs of Archbishop Sudbury and the Black Prince.*

*The tomb of Cardinal Odet de Coligny in the Trinity Chapel.*

sharply contrasted characters. Reginald Pole, the last archbishop to be a cardinal, was in office from 1556-1558. He died a few hours after his cousin, Queen Mary Tudor, and was buried in a simple brick tomb lettered, *'Depositum Cardinalis Poli'*. The 'red hat' and coat of arms which were painted on the wall at the time of his burial had both faded by the end of the nineteenth century and the large heraldic cartouche which replaced it in 1897 was the gift of Cardinal Vaughan, Roman Catholic Archbishop of Westminster. Archbishop Frederick Temple, 1897-1902, is buried in the Great Cloister. His monument here in Cornish granite was designed by W.D. Caroe and a fine bronze effigy by F.W. Pomeroy shows the Archbishop kneeling at a predieu vested in the cope he wore at the coronation of Edward VII. His gold primatial cross and coats of arms make a nice contrast with the granite monument and the elaborate wooden canopy overhead.

### The South Choir Ambulatory

The oddest tomb in the cathedral stands between two pillars on the south side of the Trinity Chapel. On examination the burial place of Odet de Coligny-Chatillon, sometime Cardinal Archbishop of Toulouse and Count Bishop of Beauvais, turns out to be little more than a pile of Tudor bricks. Born in 1517 into one of the great noble families of France, he and his brothers embraced the tenets of Calvinism and became leaders of the Huguenot party in France. In 1564 Odet married an ex-nun, the Dame de Loré and was excommunicated by Pope Pius IV and stripped of his preferments in the Church. While in England seeking help for his co-religionists from Queen Elizabeth in 1571, he came to stay in Canterbury with one of the prebendaries, John Bungay, and was lodged in the house in the Precincts still known as Meister Omers. Here he was taken ill, dying some three weeks afterwards, possibly poisoned by his valet at the instance of his many enemies, but more probably of tertian fever. An embarrassed cathedral chapter had the body brought over to the Trinity Chapel and buried in a vacant bay, expecting, no doubt, that his family would claim his body and remove it for interment in his native land. This never happened and it was not until 1952 that the heraldic cartouche on the pillar above the tomb was presented by Mr John Dickens and designed and executed by Cecil Thomas.

In the next bay to the west lies William Courtenay, archbishop from 1381 to 1396. Both tomb and effigy are in alabaster and may well be a portrait. The Archbishop has a heavy, fleshy face which suggests the arrogance of a medieval noble; at his feet is a small hound and round the tomb are niches for little figures of the kind known as 'weepers', all of which seem to have been torn out at some time. A continuous frieze of small shields runs round above the niches and there is the usual fine iron grille, perhaps to protect the tomb from the jostling of pilgrims.

No tomb in the cathedral is a more impressive example of the combined skills of the finest craftsmen of the age than that of the Black Prince Edward of Woodstock, Prince of Wales, 1330-1376. In his will he left careful instructions about the manner of his burial in the cathedral bequeathing to the priory many splendid gifts of plate and vestments. His express wish to be buried in the Chapel of Our Lady Undercroft 'at a distance of ten feet from the altar' was set aside and he lies instead in the Trinity Chapel by the spot where the Shrine once stood, in a sumptuous tomb of Purbeck marble possibly designed by his own architect Henry Yevele. Round the lid runs a brass inscription in French ending with a prayer for his soul. On the sides of the chest are enamelled coats of arms which he used in war and peace, the latter being the three ostrich feathers argent on a ground sable, which may have been the reason for him being known as 'The Black Prince'. The effigy of latten or copper-gilt shows him in full armour, with a helmet on his head and a small bulldog at his feet. Above is suspended a great carved wooden tester on which is a painting of the Holy Trinity to whom he had a special devotion: the artist is thought to have been Gilbert Prince, Master Painter to the Royal Household. Modern achievements of arms replaced the fourteenth-century originals on the iron bar over the tomb in 1954. In a glass case at the bottom of the Pilgrim Steps, just below, can be seen

133

*The Black Prince's surcoat and shield from the south ambulatory.*

his armorial jupon, his helmet with its chain fastening, the cap of maintenance with leopard crest, as well as his shield of poplar wood and gauntlets of gilded copper lined with leather. It is probable that these were never worn by the Prince but made for his funeral here, at Michaelmas 1376.

Against the opposite wall is the oldest tomb in the cathedral, that of Hubert Walter, Archbishop 1193-1205, who ruled the kingdom during the reign of Richard the Lionheart. Made of Purbeck marble it has a gabled top and resembles a metal casket adorned with gems; six fine heads are carved on front and sides, which may well be portraits of contemporaries. In 1890 when the tomb was opened in the presence of the chapter, his fully-vested body was found inside a Caen stone coffin with his name 'Hubert' engraved on a leaden plate. His pontifical vestments are now in the cathedral library and the ornaments buried with him are in the crypt treasury.

There is a tradition that after the destruction of his shrine in 1538, the remains of St Anselm were buried in the chapel that bears his name, but no stone marks the spot. The only brass in the cathedral, that commemorating Canon Holland who died in 1907, is in the floor before the altar, but the chapel is dominated by the great black marble tomb of Archbishop Simon Meopham, 1328-1333, which fills the whole of its north side. It is set in a lovely stone screen with iron gates at each end and a stone canopy overhead. In the spandrels of the tomb are carved figures of angels with symbols of the four Evangelists. In the arcaded screen are figures of little monks sitting at desks as if at work in the scriptorium of the monastery.

In the fourteenth century part of Prior Eastry's great parclose screen was removed from along the south side of the presbytery to make way for the tombs of two archbishops. That of Simon of Sudbury, 1375-1381 confronts the visitor who emerges from St Anselm's Chapel. Beheaded most brutally by Kentish rebels during the Peasants' Revolt in June 1381, his body was brought back to the cathedral and buried in an exceptionally long tomb which is surmounted by a stone canopy, vaulted like a miniature chantry chapel, and adorned with carvings of little animals. While his body lies here, his severed head can be seen preserved in the Church of St Gregory, which he built in his native town of Sudbury in Suffolk. Each year, on Christmas Day, the Mayor and Council of Canterbury come in procession to this tomb to remember his benefactions to Canterbury which included the great west gate and the Church of Holy Cross (now the city Guildhall). A sheaf of Christmas roses is placed by the Mayor in the centre niche on the ambulatory side.

In the next bay is another Purbeck marble tomb, that of John of Stratford, archbishop 1333-1349. Though he was the builder of the famous church of Holy Trinity at Stratford-on-Avon, his native town, he preferred to be buried in his cathedral church. His tomb is an early example of Perpendicular Gothic work with a fine alabaster effigy in mitre and mass vestments, a very early example of the use of this kind of stone for monumental purposes. Over the figure of the Archbishop is a little vaulted roof with a tall, elaborately pinnacled canopy enclosing all.

The third tomb on this side of the presbytery dominates the others by reason of its towering oak canopy, a magnificent piece of carpentry

elaborately carved and painted. There is no effigy, but a handsome tomb chest contains the body of John Kemp, a local boy from the township of Wye, who rose to be archbishop first of York and then of Canterbury 1452-4. He also held the office of Chancellor of the Realm and a Cardinal's hat. The chest has lost its coats of arms from the sides but has retained a brass epitaph which runs round the lid, interspersed with the 'garb' or wheatsheaf which was one of the charges in the Cardinal's arms.

Passing down the ambulatory, the reconstructed memorial of Dean Thomas Nevil, 1597-1615, can be seen in an embrasure in the wall. Once in a chapel in the nave, which is now destroyed, it displays the Dean, in choir habit with Cambridge DD hood, and his brother Alexander, in armour, both kneeling at prayer.

Under a nearby window is the only tomb of a prior of Christ Church in the cathedral, a mark of the greatness of Henry of Eastry 1285-1331, who died 'in time of Mass', having ruled his community with great wisdom for forty-six years. His effigy shows him in mitre and mass vestments lying on a handsome tomb, the cost of which is recorded as being £21 3s 4d in the priory accounts. There are traces of paint on the figure and a small canopy overhead. The canted niches at each end of the tomb once held statues of St Sythe and St Appolonia. The tomb in the next bay is now thought to be that of Walter

*The effigy of Archbishop Stratford.*

Reynolds, archbishop 1313-1328, and tutor to King Edward II. It has an arcaded front with nine niches and on it lies a mitred effigy, the head on a cushion and two dogs at its feet. The prelate carries no cross and wears no pallium over the chasuble and, for this reason, Dr F. Woodman has suggested that it might be the effigy of a prior (perhaps Richard Oxenden who died in 1338), moved up from St Michael's Chapel and laid on top of Reynold's tomb. Several tablets and memorials moved from the same chapel more recently can now be seen on the side walls at the west end of the ambulatory. The most conspicuous is a female bust in a kind of Baroque reredos to Ann Mills, telling us that she died in 1714, aged 20, being endowed with 'the whole choir of Christian virtues!'

## The Crypt

Down in the crypt we find the tombs of two noble ladies who were on familiar terms with the monks in the later Middle Ages. By the altar of Our Lady Undercroft lies Lady Joan of Burghesh, later the wife of Sir John de Mohun of Dunster, whom she married in 1340. Her tomb, prepared before her death in 1404, shows her resting under a canopy with her head on two tasselled cushions. She is wearing a sleeveless tunic with a jewelled girdle, her head coroneted and a lion at her feet. A few yards away in St Gabriel's Chapel lies Lady

Elizabeth Trivet, who was in high favour at the court of Richard II. She is buried in a plain tomb and her effigy shows an elderly lady in hood, mantle and long girdled gown with her head on a cushion supported by angels and a dog at her feet. She died in 1433 leaving a considerable legacy to the priory.

Opposite the door of the French Church is the very elaborate monument of Cardinal John Morton. Archbishop from 1486 to 1500, he was actually buried under a large slab, once covered by a brass, before the altar of Our Lady Undercroft. An effigy of the Archbishop in mitre and mass vestments lies on the usual chest with small figures of clerks (perhaps monks) in fur almuces kneeling by him. These might be supposed to be his secretaries, or perhaps the priests who, it is recorded were paid 3s 4d a week to sing the Office of the Dead daily for the repose of his soul. At the east end of the tomb, against a pillar is a painting of the Annunciation, at which he is gazing, which was restored in 1947 by Professor Tristram. Despite the mutilation of much of the statuary at the hands of later vandals it still remains a rich and colourful memorial with carvings of saints, one of which, St Christopher, is more or less intact, though the cardinals' hats and Tudor portcullises have been battered. Most prominent among these badges is his rebus, a mor (or hawk) on a barrel (or tun) which also appears, carved in stone on the great central tower which is his noblest memorial.

### St Michael's Chapel

St Michael's Chapel in the south-west transept has a fine collection of tombs and monuments spanning several centuries. The earliest and simplest is a stone coffin inscribed only with a floriated cross which holds the remains of Stephen Langton archbishop from 1207 to 1228. Eight years after the translation of St Thomas's Body to the shrine in the retro-choir, which was the climax of Langton's career, his own tomb was placed in the apse of the Romanesque Chapel of St Michael. But, after two centuries, the construction of a new chapel in the fashionable Perpendicular style entailed the building of a square east end into which the whole stone tomb would not fit, so the wall was made to 'stride over' it. His 'feet' stick out into the churchyard, protected by a coping stone off which the rain runs: shabby treatment for so great a man's mortal remains!

The person responsible for this lies in the centre of the chapel in great funereal pomp. Lady Margaret Holland with her first husband,

*Effigies from St Michael's Chapel.*

*The pet dog of the Duke of Clarence.*

the Beaufort Earl of Somerset on her left and his successor, the Plantagenet Duke Thomas of Clarence on her right. She had them both interred, temporarily after their deaths in the place now occupied by Dean Wotton's tomb in the Trinity Chapel. When the new chapel and tomb were ready, at the request of Henry VI the monks allowed the burial of all three of these grand personages in the new chapel, which was consecrated in December 1439. Richard Beke, the master mason, was the designer of this very large tomb with the alabaster figures of the Duchess and her consorts. They are in full armour, the Earl with a falcon at his feet and the Duke with a large hound for his feet to rest on, while the Duchess is in rich robes covered by a mantle, a wimpled coronet on her head and two little dogs at her feet. The figures are carved in great detail, even the pins which hold the Duchess's wimple in place are carefully executed. All around are knightly figures of the sevententh century in impressive tombs: Colonel Prudde, killed at Maastricht in 1632; Sir Thomas Thornhurst killed at the siege of La Rochelle, 1627, with his wife lying below and their children carved on the front of the tomb.

The wife of Sir Richard Baker of Sissinghurst, a Thornhurst before her marriage, lies on the next tomb in a ruff and farthingale. She died in 1609 and the trio of Thornhurst monuments is completed with a hanging one to Dame Dorothy, a severe looking matron kneeling at a predieu who died in 1620. Almost overwhelming in its Baroque grandeur is a great monument, on the right side of the chapel altar which commemorates a local hero, Sir George Rooke, who was Admiral of the Fleet which captured Gibraltar in 1703. A bust of the Admiral in a periwig attributed to Edward Stanton, is the centrepiece, with some, attractive reliefs below showing men of war with guns firing in action, as well as a long Latin epitaph recording his exploits and his three marriages. Sir George was a citizen of Canterbury and died in the city in 1708.

Near the chapel gate is another large monument adorned with shields and trophies of arms to the memory of a contemporary of Sir George, Colonel Godfrey, one of the staff of Prince George of Denmark, consort of Queen Anne in 1712. For many years the Warriors' Chapel of St Michael has been the memorial chapel of the Buffs, the Royal East Kent Regiment, and a Book of Remembrance illuminated by Graily Hewitt stands on a handsome lectern by Bainbridge Reynolds with the names of many thousands of officers and men of the Regiment who fell in the two World Wars. A page of this book is turned over every day at 11am. Memorials to the Queen's Own Rifles of Canada and the Royal Queen's Lancers, as well as a book recording the names of all those civilians who perished in Canterbury during the second World War are kept in this part of the church.

Many regimental memorials, and tablets to individual soldiers of the Victorian era are ranged along the south wall of the nave. Of other worthies commemorated the most unusual monument is that of Robert Berkeley, who died in 1614, son of Sir Maurice Berkeley, standard bearer of Henry VIII and successive Tudor monarchs. This Jacobean tablet is notable for a charming rhyming epitaph attributed to Bishop Henry King of Chichester. The best piece of sculpture here is by Rysbrack to John Symson and is dated 1732. Another mock-medieval tomb commemorates William Grant Broughton, an old King's School boy who went out as a missionary to Australia, becoming its first Anglican bishop. On a visit to England he died in 1853 and was buried here; his effigy in rochet and chimere is the work of John Graham Lough who was much admired in the early Victorian days. Portrait medallions of Dean Farrar (1903) and Margaret Babington, the inimitable steward of the Friends of the Cathedral for thirty years (1928-1958) are at the west end of the nave.

On the wall under the south-west tower are listed the names of the deans and priors who have presided over the life and worship of Christ Church Cathedral in Canterbury for well over a thousand years.

# Chapter Six

# THE ORNAMENTS, FURNITURE AND FITTINGS

Entering THE CATHEDRAL Precincts on the south-west side by the Christ Church Gate the visitor is instantly confronted by its fine wooden doors set up immediately after the Restoration of Charles II in 1660. The original doors, which would have dated back to early Tudor times, had been torn off and burnt by the Puritans in 1643 as part of a great assault on this gate. The attack culminated in the destruction of the statue of Christ which once stood in the niche over the gateway and was torn down by ropes after it had been used for target practice and barbarously mutilated. In a memorandum in the handwriting of William Somner, antiquary and auditor to the Dean and Chapter, written in about 1662 he records how 'the Churches guardian, her fair and strong Gates, were betimes turned off the hooks and burned'. The new gates are carved with the arms of Archbishop Juxon, 1660-3, and those of the Dean and Chapter, all in a classical setting of grotesque heads, scrolls, and festoons of fruit and flowers as was popular at this period all over Europe. The arms of the new dean, Thomas Turner, who had returned from exile with Charles II, are carved on the small wooden door of the postern.

### The Nave

If there is no welcoming figure of Christ over the Christ Church Gate to welcome the Canterbury pilgrims of today, they will find a very attractive modern one inside the south-west door carved in afrarmosia, an African wood, by W. Day, a local sculptor, and set up to commemorate the eight hundredth anniversary of the murder of Becket in 1970. The wooden screens of this vestibule area are made up of fragments of carved woodwork of the late-seventeenth century,

*The seventeenth-century font in the nave.*

dismantled in Victorian times but still preserved in various parts of the cathedral. At the west end of the nave, at the entrance to St Augustine's Chapel, has been erected in recent years a lofty baldachino, all that remains of a magnificent wooden throne given by Dr Tenison, Archbishop from 1695 to 1716. It is almost certain that this throne was designed by Nicholas Hawksmoor and carved by Grinling Gibbons. It was erected in the choir in 1705 in the traditional position on the south side, with its fluted Corinthian columns and linking arch surmounted by a mitre. Regrettably, with a change of

*Grilles from the nave arcade.*

taste, this was removed in 1844 in favour of the present mock-Gothic stone throne.

Only a few feet away in the third bay from the west is the unusual and impressive font dating from the Laudian revival. The gift of one of the canons, John Warner, in 1639, it commemorated his preferment to the See of Rochester two years earlier. There does not seem to have been a permanent font for use in monastic times: since there was no parish attached to the cathedral, baptisms would have been infrequent. Shortly before the Dissolution, Henry VIII sent to Canterbury to borrow a silver portable font for a baptism at

*The arms of the chapter in the seventeenth-century iron gate of the Chapel of Our Lady Martyrdom.*

Greenwich Palace and, not suprisingly, it was never returned. The earliest date in the cathedral registers for a baptism is in December 1564 so one can only suppose that a temporary font must have done duty until 1639. Only three years later the new font was smashed by Puritan soldiers, and posterity has to thank the courage and devotion of William Somner for its survival, since he collected the broken pieces and hid them in his house until the Restoration when the font was set up again with new figures in 1662.

The font thus restored only remained in the nave for 125 years. In 1789 a great clearance of the nave took place, gravestones, indents of brasses and other monuments of the past being ruthlessly swept away, and the font was banished to the upper storey of the Water Tower which was often thereafter referred to as the baptistry. It was returned to its ancient place in the nave in 1896, where happily it still remains. It stands on a marble plinth, with four figures of the Evangelists in white marble, their traditional emblems at their feet, being placed around the stem. This is surmounted by a shallow, octagonal and fluted bowl on which is a two-storied wooden cover adorned with figures of the twelve Apostles, eight on the lower storey and four on that above. The cover rises to a pinnacle on which stands a figure of Christ blessing little children and is raised by a metal pulley which hangs from a bracket bearing the royal arms of Charles II. The odious Puritan fanatic 'Blue Dick' Culmer inveighed against 'those tempting images in the place of divine Worship, against the Law of God and the Doctrine of the Church of England' and we can presume that he had a considerable share in damaging the font. By contrast the gentler Puritan, Mistress Celia Fiennes, visiting Canterbury in 1697 noted the font with rather more approval, describing it as 'well carved and painted and gilded, the bottom is white and grey marble with white marble statues round the stem to the foote, the top is made in a pirimidy carved and painted'.

The only other object of furniture in the nave worthy of note is the handsome pulpit of carved and painted wood designed in 1898 by the great Gothic Revival architect, George Bodley, in memory of Dr R Payne-Smith, a distinguished oriental scholar and educationalist who was dean from 1871 to 1895. The pulpit which is in Perpendicular Gothic style, has carvings of the Crucifixion and Annunciation around it, a canopy above, and two figures in cope and mitre representing St Augustine of Canterbury and St Gregory on either side of its stairway.

While the present arrangement of altar and sanctuary furnishings in the nave is simple, modern and calls for no particular comment, the tall wrought iron grilles in the nave arcade between pulpit and sanctuary are of fine craftsmanship. These were given in 1938 by Mr and Mrs Dickins of Croydon. A very fine seventeenth-century gate of wrought iron leads from the Martyrdom Transept into the Lady Chapel. The arms of the Dean and Chapter which form part of the design recall the fact that this was once called the Deans' Chapel because so many post-Reformation deans are interred here. Under the east window of this chapel hangs a brightly coloured tapestry woven by Michael Halsey: this and the simple altar table and lectern

OPPOSITE: *The Madonna and Child in the Chapel of Our Lady Martyrdom.*

of wood made by the cathedral carpenters were placed here in 1980 in memory of Canon Thomas Prichard.

Hanging from the vault above is a bronze pyx for reservation of the Blessed Sacrament and the Holy Oils for the sick and dying, the work of Leslie Durbin, given in memory of Canon Herbert Waddams in 1981. In the same year the lovely statue of the Madonna and Child was installed in an empty niche on the north side of the altar, executed in bronze by the Benedictine sculptress, Sister Concordia, Prioress of Minster in Thanet.

### The Western Crypt

Descending into the western crypt we see another example of her work in a niche over the altar of Our Lady Undercroft: a majestic bronze figure of the Virgin and Child, which to many people enhances the devotional atmosphere of this chapel which is much used by the cathedral community for vigils of prayer, as well as for weddings and funerals. In an embrasure in the north wall a few yards away is a splendid statue, carved in wood and painted in gold and colours, depicting Thomas Becket in full pontificals given by the Church of Sweden to the cathedral in 1930. The statue is a fine replica of a fifteenth-century original now in a museum in Stockholm, but originally made for the Swedish Church of Skepptuna dedicated to St Thomas soon after his murder in 1170. The sculptor is now thought to have been Bernt Notke, 1440-1517, a German artist from Lubeck who worked most of his life in Sweden.

On the wall of the Chapel of St Mary Magdalene is a small alabaster panel dating from the later Middle Ages depicting the Entombement of Christ, probably the work of the Nottingham School of Carvers c. 1350.

At the west end of the eastern crypt are two ranges of carved stalls, ten on each side, the gift of Mr and Mrs Dickins. These are fine examples of modern woodwork with much carving of ornament in Renaissance style. They were placed originally at the east end of the nave in 1938 at the same time as the iron grilles and were moved here as recently as 1977 for use at the weekday services.

An impressive table in Italian walnut and ebony stands on a raised platform composed largely of medieval encaustic tiles in the apse of the Jesus Chapel at the east end of the crypt. This was set up in December 1880 as the high altar of the cathedral, a position which it held until 1977 when a reordering of the sanctuary arrangements led

OPPOSITE: *The wrought iron gate of the Pulpitum Screen.*

to its removal and its eventual placing here. The work of the Victorian firm of Messrs Farmer and Brindley, it has a series of mosaic panels of angels set into the front which are usually covered by a handsome frontal, worked by the Kilburn Sisters in 1895, to the design of the London firm of Heaton and Baker.

## The Choir

Returning to the upper part of the church we enter the choir through the fine iron gates of the pulpitum screen: these are of an unusual design and date from the early years of the fifteenth century. Perhaps it is worth noticing here a curious abrasion of the stone-work inside the screen door on the left hand side where a Holy Water sprinkler on a chain once hung for the use of the monks entering the choir for Divine Service. The constant swing of the chain has left behind marks on the stone which still remain four and a half centuries later. A survey of the choir from this point gives the impression of rather a mass of dark woodwork and a closer examination reveals all these stalls and pews to be of late Victorian craftsmanship. The monastic stalls which may well have had misericords but did not have canopies, as is the case in the choirs of Winchester, Gloucester and Chester where the monastic stalls are still in use, were removed in 1704 to be replaced by much wainscoting and pewing. Comfortable as these pews may have been before the days of central heating, after little more than a century and a half they were swept away in favour of the present stalls and pews, the work of Messrs Farmer and Brindley under the general direction of Sir Gilbert Scott in 1879. The rear stalls are all equipped with misericords in a medieval style and there is a wealth of fine carving on the poppy heads at the end of each range of pews. Excellent though this work is of its kind, it cannot bear comparison with the twelve splendid stalls for the Dean and Chapter which are set against the pulpitum screen at the west end of the choir. These were the work of Roger Davis of London, 'citizen and joiner' and were set up here in 1682 at a cost of £320. They represent English woodwork of the period at its best and we must be thankful that they escaped destruction by Sir Gilbert Scott who wished to substitute mock Gothic stalls of his own design but was happily overruled by the Dean and Chapter. Among the luxuriant carvings of fruit and flowers can be seen the Royal Arms of Charles II and those of Archbishop Sheldon and the Dean and Chapter.

At the other end of the choir is a plain stone pulpit, the gift of Dean

OPPOSITE: *Dr Bargrave's table, now kept in the Norman Water Tower.*

ABOVE: *Seventeenth-century return stalls from the choir.*

*The thirteenth-century mosaic pavement behind the High Altar.*

Lyall, in 1846, designed by Mr Butterfield who was engaged at this time in the building of St Augustine's College.

Nearby stands the great brass eagle lectern which replaces one given by Prior Goldstone in Tudor times and destroyed by the Puritans. This was the work of William Burroughes in 1663 and cost £59. The eagle perches on a ball and the pedestal on which it rests stands on three sitting lions. Until the middle of the eighteenth century this stood between the choir stalls facing south. Exiled for some hundred years in the cathedral library, it was replaced in its present position in the choir in 1847.

The great stone seat with its spired canopy, in the traditional position on the south side of the choir, is that in which the archbishops are enthroned and normally sit as bishops of the Diocese of Canterbury. Designed by George Austin and given by Archbishop Howley in 1844, it replaced Archbishop Tenison's wooden throne, the grandiose remains of which we have seen at the west end of the nave.

Of much greater importance is the venerable stone chair of Purbeck marble — the *Sedes Marmorea* — which now stands at the top of the steps behind the High Altar. Here from time immemorial archbishops have been enthroned as Primates of All England either in person or often by proxy. Sometimes known, erroneously, as St Augustine's Chair it may well have replaced an earlier Patriarchal

*The mosaic pavement and the back of the archbishops' marble chair.*

Chair destroyed in the fire of 1174. There is a tradition that it was made for Archbishop Stephen Langton and placed where it now stands in time for the great ceremonies of the Translation of St Thomas in July 1220. Six centuries later as a result of a re-ordering of the sanctuary in 1825, it was banished to the Corona, and the High Altar moved up the steps to take its place, so that for the next hundred years enthronements of archbishops took place 'off stage'. In 1928 the chair was moved down and placed on top of the steps in front of the pulpitum screen for the enthronement of Cosmo Lang and this practice was repeated at subsequent enthronements down to that of Donald Coggan. Having been restored to its ancient place in 1977 it was not necessary to move it from here for the magnificent ceremony for the enthronement of Robert Runcie on Lady Day 1980.

A curious survival of long-forgotten ritual can be discovered with some difficulty on the pillar to the east side of Cardinal Kemp's tomb: a bracket shaped like a castle from which a veil was suspended across the sanctuary during Lent. The corresponding bracket on the opposite side has disappeared. In 1511 Prior Goldstone II gave a superb set of Flemish tapestries with scenes of the life and death of the Blessed Virgin Mary to be hung on festivals along the south side of the choir above the monastic stalls, while at the same time one of the monks, Richard Dering the cellarer, gave a similar set of scenes from the life of our Lord Jesus. These were all removed during the Commonwealth and sold by order of Cromwell's government in 1656 in Paris to the Chapter of Aix en Provence for 1200 écus. Some of them can still be seen hanging over the stalls of the canons of that cathedral. The kneelers of the aluminium rails round the High Altar are pleasant examples of modern needlework representing the flowers that have been chosen as the individual emblems of the different states that make up the USA. They were embroidered by members of the Needlepoint Committee of the Cathedral of Washington DC and presented at the Friends' Festival in 1961.

The cathedral is rich in brass candelabra: no less than six of these hang at this east end of the church, two in each of the transepts, one in St Anselm's Chapel and one over the site of the shrine in the Trinity Chapel. In 1692 Sir Anthony Aucher gave the first of these to light the middle of the choir, and his example was followed in 1726 by Dr Edward Tenison, one of the prebendaries who gave another to hang in the presbytery. A third was the gift of Dr Shuckford, another prebendary, in 1747 'to light the way between the vestry and the quire'. Passing now into the south ambulatory, the visitor will notice the curious oval altar of marble with its curved rails, dedicated in 1951 and designed by Stephen Dykes Bower, in the Chapel of St John the Evangelist as a memorial to Archbishop William Temple, 1942-1944.

In the Chapel of St Anselm is a modern altar-piece, a Calvary in Australian silver-bean wood and silver, given by Mr John Dickins, the donor of the iron grilles in the nave and the stalls in the eastern crypt. The Calvary, which was dedicated in 1951, was the work of Andar Meszarcs, a Hungarian sculptor, who settled in Australia as a refugee during the Second World War. After his death his widow presented to the cathedral a beautiful gift in memory of her husband, his fourteen Stations of the Cross in bronze, at present in a case in the north ambulatory.

*Aries the Ram from the thirteenth-century French pavement at the west end of Trinity Chapel.*

### The Trinity Chapel

Ascending the great medieval staircase to the Trinity Chapel, usually known as the Pilgrim Steps, we see high up in the vault over the shrine area a crescent of gilded wood of foreign origin about which there has been much controversy. George Austin, the cathedral surveyor in the first half of the nineteenth century, thought it was probably a trophy of victory of the Cross over the Crescent brought back by the Crusaders, who had a special devotion to St Thomas, after their victory over the Saracens at Acre under the leadership of Richard Coeur de Lion. He suggested that it was one of a number of trophies such as flags, horsetails etc. hung up here at the time of the Translation in 1220, of which this alone survives. Another view is that this is all that remains of a lost painting of the Blessed Virgin Mary standing on the crescent moon and set above the shrine which contained the mortal remains of the Martyr Saint whose Patron she is known to have been.

The pavement of the chapel has been described as 'one of the most, perhaps the most, splendid ever laid in medieval England, certainly the most splendid and expensive pavement of which so great an area remains'. At the top of the steps is a fine mosaic pavement of Opus Alexandrinum work flanked on either side by a series of French roundels from the city of St Omer in northern France, all this linking the Marble Chair of the Archbishops with the area once occupied by the shrine of St Thomas. All this paved area was probably laid in the decade that led up to the Translation of the body of St Thomas to this chapel in 1220. The mosaic pavement is of Italian work of a kind still to be seen in the churches of Rome and known as Cosmati work after the family responsible for this kind of pavement. It has been described as 'a lozenge in a quatrefoil, in a square, in a much bigger lozenge overlapping four circles' and it was most probably imported to adorn the area near the shrine at the behest of Archbishop Stephen Langton whose sojourn in Rome as cardinal would have made him familiar with this kind of contemporary paving. The roundels on either side of the mosaic are arranged in groups of three, eighteen on either side, representing the twelve signs of the Zodiac and twelve months of the year and seven virtues and vices with some fantastic beasts as well. Executed in yellow oolite, these were probably brought over at the request of the monks who spent the years 1207 to 1213 at the Abbey of St Bertin in St Omer during the prolonged quarrel between Pope Innocent III and King John over the appointment of an archbishop in succession to Hubert Walter. Six other roundels can be seen at the east end of the pavement, composed of a mixture of Purbeck and Bethersden marble with some rose-pink marble of Italian origin of the kind of which the shrine itself was composed, which may well have been used to make good the pavement after the demolition of 1538. Following the great commemoration of the eight hundredth anniversary of the martyrdom in 1970 the Cathedral Chapter had an inscription in brass letters inserted in the midst of the pavement which reads 'The Shrine of Thomas Becket Archbishop and Martyr stood here 1220 to 1538' and on this spot a candle burns daily.

### The Corona

The Corona Chapel also has a medieval pavement, much of it composed of thirteenth-century Purbeck marble with a platform two steps up on which would have stood the altar where was preserved 'a part of the head of St Thomas the Martyr' throughout the Middle Ages. A modern altar now stands on this platform vested in a frontal designed by Joyce Conwy Evans and behind this are four roundels similar to those from St Omer at the west end of the chapel. A square section of encaustic tiles can be seen on the left side of the altar and many tiles similar to these can be seen in different parts of the

cathedral, notably in the Jesus Chapel of the crypt as well as the
Norman Vestiarium and the wax chamber beneath the High Altar
which are not open to the public. Recent research suggest that these
were made in the late thirteenth century at a 'tile factory' on the
outskirts of Canterbury, an area now known as Tyler Hill.

A peep through the lovely fifteenth-century wooden screen of the
Chantry of Henry IV reveals a charming altar with cross, candlesticks,
frontal and dorsal designed by Professor Tristram in 1931 when the
chapel was restored to use again after nearly 400 years. On the green
curtain above the altar are embroidered figures representing St
Edward the Confessor and the Beggar (really St John the Evangelist in
disguise) holding the ring given to him by the King, one of the many
legends surrounding the figure of the Saxon monarch who was for
many centuries England's Patron Saint.

In the north choir ambulatory the visitor will note first the hanging
clock on the west wall of the north-east transept, conspicuous for its
long pendulum with a head like a blazing sun at its foot and on each
side 'quarter jack' figures — a monk on the right symbolizing the
Church and a knight on the left representing the State. No-one knows
where the clock came from or how old it is, though it is said to be a
copy of an old Dutch clock and has been in the cathedral for at least a
century. Near the west end of the ambulatory is the oldest door in the
building, opening on to a staircase which once led up to the Chapel of
St Blaise which was demolished in the fifteenth century. Expert
opinion now considers the woodwork of the door to go back to the
rebuilding of the choir in the time of William of Sens in about 1175,
while the ironwork is a good deal older and may belong to the time of
Lanfranc, having been re-used here after the great fire of 1174.

### The Organ

From this point in the ambulatory one can look across to the south
triforium and see the pipes of the main cathedral organ which have
been in this position for the last century. There are records of organs
and organists in medieval times, and in 1540 it is recorded that 'a pair
of organs' was among the furnishings of the cathedral. Organs at this
period were small affairs with pipes but no pedals. A rough idea of
what they looked like can still be seen in the cathedral library where a
portable organ, with the arms of Dean Bargrave 1625 to 1642 painted
on the front, is preserved. The Puritan soldiers, in many palaces dealt
harshly with these instruments which they called 'boxes of whistles'
and treated with the same barbarity as the stained glass windows and
the statues. At the Restoration the Dean and Chapter lost little time in
refurnishing their cathedral with an organ, the chosen builder being

Lancelot Pease of Cambridge who in 1663 set up a new organ of two manuals and nineteen stops. They cannot have felt that they got value for money, for only twenty years later they commissioned another organ from the famous builder 'Father' Bernard Smith who set up the instrument in a handsome case in a loft in the north ambulatory. This had only fourteen stops, one of which was a trumpet and considered to be something of a novelty. This was obviously a better bargain since it lasted until 1752 when it was rebuilt and a third manual added. By this time the Chapter had learnt to employ the best craftsman and in 1784 they called in Samuel Green, a builder of high reputation who rebuilt the organ and moved it to the pulpitum screen, the loft in the aisle disappearing in due course. In 1827 the pipe work was moved to the south triforium and a new console set up in a loft in the aisle below from which the organist could look down upon his singers, a pedal board being added for the first time to the three manuals.

In 1886 Henry Willis, the greatest builder of the Victorian era, set up what is, in essence, the present instrument, with four manuals and pedals and fifty-two speaking stops including two tubas on the solo organ. Early in the twentieth century five new stops were added to the pedal and choir departments by the firm of Norman and Beard, then in charge of the instrument, but it was always felt by musicians that the organ suffered from the peculiar placing of the pipes in the south triforium. On the eve of the Second World War the firm of Henry Willis was invited to rebuild the organ but their works in Brixton were damaged during the war and it was not possible for the rebuilt organ to return to the cathedral until 1948. The console was now placed on the pulpitum screen and the pipes returned to their former position in the south triforium but the organ still remained unsatisfactory both to play and to hear, and after another unsuccessful attempt in 1968, the firm of Noel Mander was commissioned to carry out a radical rebuild and rearrangement of the pipes in 1978. When the organ was heard again in the autumn of 1979, equipped with a handsome new console there were some startling and impressive changes. The main instrument now had 54 speaking stops, many of them newly-arranged in three manuals, the solo department now being combined with the unenclosed choir. All the pipes in the triforium had now been brought forward to project more tone into both choir and nave, a rearrangement which has been entirely satisfactory. Most impressive of all the improvements to the organ has been the creation of a new 'chorus' of six stops in a beautiful case

OPPOSITE: *The organ case in the north nave aisle together with the seventeenth-century bust of Orlando Gibbons.*

placed on the north wall of the nave near the monument of Orlando Gibbons. It is played from the great manual on the pulpitum screen and when first heard, at the enthronement of Robert Runcie, it was realized that this addition would revolutionize services in the nave.

In addition to this magnificent instrument, the cathedral possesses five small organs. One by Peter Collins of St Albans was presented in 1975 and is a one manual instrument ideally suited for accompanying Baroque or Early Church music, while a charming eighteenth-century one-manual organ given by Michael Galpin in *c.* 1962 normally stands in the Trinity Chapel for use on the rare occasions when services are sung there. In addition there are three organs in the crypt. At the west end is a small one-manual by Noel Mander. The remaining two organs are by the firm of F.E. Browne, both two-manual with pedals: the one in the eastern crypt bearing the date 1962; and that in the Huguenot Church being a much older instrument of 1889. A beautifully illuminated list of cathedral organists whose names are known from 1407 to the present day can be seen at the top of the steps leading from the south-west transept to the choir ambulatory.

## The Bells

The cathedral, which now has twenty-one bells in regular use, hung in three of its towers, has had bells of varying sizes from very early times and may even have had a bell cast by St Dunstan in the tenth century since he is reputed to have been a craftsman in the field of metalwork. From Norman times onwards a number of bells were hung in a detached campanile standing on a mound near the south-west transept. On 21 May 1382 a severe earthquake severely damaged this tower and shook down the six bells hanging in it which were used for announcing services or marking special feasts. The campanile itself was finally demolished in the middle of the seventeeth century but the mound survives and can still be seen in 'South Close'.

Early in the fifteenth century the Romanesque central tower, known as the 'Angel Steeple' was also in use as a belfry and there was a ring of five bells in it given jointly by Archbishop Arundel and Prior Chillenden. The Angel Steeple was demolished to make room for a new great central tower in Perpendicular style as early as 1433, though this was not completed until 1504 because of lack of funds. Any idea of using this new tower as a belfry was abandoned for structural reasons, as the great strainer arches, so prominent inside the building, make clear to this day.

The most ancient of all the cathedral bells now in use, known as

'Bell Harry', hangs in a frame on top of the leads of the tower to which it gives its name. This name is probably derived from a medieval bell given by Prior Henry of Eastry and is the work of a Kentish bellfounder Joseph Hatch of Ulcombe. Cast in 1635 and weighing eight hundredweight (400 kilograms), it is operated electrically and rings each weekday for the morning services and every night for curfew from 8.55 to 9pm, after which the gates of the Precincts are closed for the night. The south-west tower came into its own in the middle of the nineteenth century when a clock was placed in this steeple in 1855 and a peal of bells, in good order, was rung for the first time on Christmas Eve the following year. On the leads of this tower, to strike the hours, was placed the splendid bell called Great Dunstan, weighing 62 hundredweight (3,100 kilograms) and cast in the Precincts in 1762. Until 1980 it served as a clock bell only and was occasionally tolled as a 'passing bell'. In the tower below were the smaller bells which formed the ring, gradually increasing in number until by the year 1900 there were twelve, five of which were used as quarter chimes and from 1897 onwards rang out a special chime composed by the Precentor, the Reverend F.J.O. Helmore, based on Gregorian tones.

In 1980 the decision was made to scrap most of the bells then in use, in order to have a completely new ring. This was cast in 1981 in the bell foundry in Whitechapel by the famous firm of Mears and Stainbank. On Sunday, 19 July, fourteen new bells, arranged carefully on the floor of the nave just inside the west door, were solemnly blessed and 'baptized' by Archbishop Runcie being given names, according to ancient custom, many having been borne by previous cathedral bells. The names of the bells are Simon, Crundale, Alphege, Thomas, Mary, Ethelbert, Anselm, Ernulf, Blaise, John, Lanfranc, Gabriel and Augustine, the last in the ring being Trinity, the tenor which weighs over 34 hundredweight (1,700 kilograms). These bells were cast largely from the metal of the seven bells of the previous ring, all given by private individuals or corporate bodies, several by the Friends of the Cathedral, on whose annual festival they were dedicated. The galvanized steel frame was the gift of the Woolwich Building Society and was in action for the first time on All Hallows Eve, 1981. At the same time the five clock bells together with Great Dunstan were installed in the north west tower in a frame given by the Anglia Building Society. Great Dunstan was hung for the first time for slow swinging, and his voice was heard booming out over the city before Evensong on Sunday, 15 November 1981.

# Chapter Seven

# THE PAINTINGS, PLATE
# AND BOOKS

THE MURAL PAINTINGS of the twelfth century in the cathedral are unique in their way and unsurpassed in European medieval art. These splendid works, all that survive of a great scheme which must have made the Romanesque cathedral glorious for half a century until the fire of 1174, are to be found in the chapel of St Anselm in the south choir ambulatory and in its undercroft, the Chapel of St Gabriel in the crypt, a part of the building which escaped fire damage in some miraculous way.

*The Paintings in St Anselm's Chapel*

These paintings were probably executed during the primacy of St Thomas, who was consecrated in 1162 and martyred in 1170. They are all that now illustrate the admiring words of the chronicler William of Malmesbury, who wrote of 'the many coloured pictures that led the wandering eye to the very summit of the ceiling'. To see the famous painting of St Paul one has to look up in the small apsidal sanctuary of St Anselm's Chapel on the north side. There is the great Apostle of the Gentiles, in a white tunic against a blue ground, shaking off the viper into the fire after the shipwreck which landed him and his company on the shores of Malta. St Paul holds a bunch of faggots in his hand and is barefoot; he bends over towards the fire which is burning in the right hand corner of the painting. This was only discovered during the restoration of the chapel in 1888. It is thought that there was originally a companion figure of St Peter on the opposite side, for the chapel was dedicated originally to St Peter and St Paul, and it only became known as St Anselm's Chapel after the burial of the great Archbishop here in 1109. The painting of St Peter must have perished with others of the same period in the course of time. That of St Paul survived because, soon after the completion of

*A Romanesque wall painting from St Gabriel's Chapel in the crypt.*

the chapel in the twelfth century, an internal buttress was inserted to strengthen the fabric. The painting was concealed behind this for some seven centuries and then emerged as one of the great masterpieces of the Romanesque age.

## The Chapel of St Gabriel

More extensive are the paintings which are to be found in the apsidal sanctuary and the western part of the nave vault of St Gabriel's Chapel. Christ sits in majesty, with angels surrounding him over the

163

*The painted vaulting of Our Lady Undercroft Chapel.*

altar, looking somewhat like the figures of the Pantocrator which appear in Byzantine art in the domes of Orthodox Churches. Below, in the soffit of the arch, are figures of the angels of the Seven Churches of Asia, with St John writing his Apocalypse in the eighth space. On the north wall of the chapel are scenes from the story of the birth of St John the Baptist: the Archangel Gabriel appears to Zacharias at the altar of incense in the Temple; Zacharias points to his tongue to indicate to the crowd outside that he is dumb; the birth of the Baptist and his naming as John at the insistence of his father, Zacharias. Opposite, the angel appears to Mary to announce the forthcoming birth of Jesus; Mary visits Elizabeth; Jesus is born in the stable at Bethlehem; and the angels announce this to the shepherds in the fields.

On either side of the entrance to the sanctuary are the angel guardians. Two figures of six-winged seraphim stand on wheels. On the vaulting over the arches are Trees of Life such as St John saw 'in the midst of the Paradise of God'. In the western vault the painting is not in such good condition. In the north-west bay are medallions with figures of bishops and small medallions with demi figures of kings with sceptres and crowns, angels holding books and prophets with inscribed scrolls.

The apse of the Chapel of St Gabriel was walled-in during the last years of the twelfth century, not long after the paintings were finished. This was probably done for structural reasons, though the monks may have wanted somewhere to hide their treasures during their exile in France at the time of King John. The wall remained in position until the nineteenth century when a door was opened in it giving access to the apse. The wall was finally demolished in 1950 and more paintings were discovered under the arches and on the central pillar which supports the arch. It is to this walling-up that we owe the survival of a considerable amount of painting, eight centuries old, in such relatively good condition. There were also paintings on the vault of the Trinity Chapel, executed probably in the early thirteenth century, but these were sadly destroyed in the middle of the nineteenth century.

## The Chapel of Our Lady Undercroft

Only a few yards away from St Gabriel's Chapel is the Chapel of Our Lady Undercroft where there is much fifteenth-century painting on the vault and east wall. Tristram describes the painting on the vault as originally representing 'a firmament with constellations of suns, moons and stars, composed of minute mirrors set at different angles to reflect the light from burning candles, on a ground now black but originally deep blue in colour'. Even today traces of this exciting scheme of decoration can be seen and enjoyed. More striking is the heraldic decoration on the wall on either side of the altar. Here are some thirty-eight shields of arms of the time of Henry VI, most likely representing the donors of the money spent on the work of adorning the chapel, just as the arms in the Great Cloister serve a similar purpose of commemorating the generosity of the benefactors. Among the coats of arms are those of Archbishops Arundel, Chichele and Stafford, as well as the coats of the Black Prince, Queen Joan of Navarre and many of the prominent noblemen of the age who had some connection with the cathedral and its priory.

## St Andrew's Chapel

In St Andrew's Chapel is a good deal of ornamental painting. The earliest consists of an elaborate geometric design in bright blue and red, which appears on the eastern arch. Another layer, again of the twelfth century, and covering much of the rest of this Romanesque chapel is a masonry design common at this period in which courses of stone are represented in paint. Over this is a later vine pattern and painted hangings, in red on a white background; while on the west wall is a layer of whitewash decorated with fleur de lys and small rosettes. This area of the cathedral has been under restoration for some time and will shortly be open to visitors.

## The Jesus Chapel

In the Jesus Chapel, the undercroft of the Corona, is a lovely Gothic vault, with a central boss, all erected in the last decades of the twelfth century as part of the extension of the cathedral after the fire of 1174. Professor Tristram described the painting here as 'remains of a light ornamental treatment probably of late fourteenth century date consisting of a simple masonry pattern with horizontal bands of zig-zag ornament and a diaper of M.s (for Mary) and I.s (for Jesus); each initial surmounted by a crown'. Until recently all that could be seen were pale letters of a greyish colour, but in the years 1980 to 1982 a sensitive and imaginative restoration of this vault took place which culminated in the painting of the central boss in red and gold, as it was in medieval times.

This work was followed by the restoration of a large wall painting of the legend of St Eustace (or Hubert), patron of huntsmen who was converted, when hunting on Good Friday, by seeing a stag approach with a crucifix between its antlers. The mural, which bears some resemblance to a tapestry, fills a large embrasure next to the Bible Windows in the north choir ambulatory. It is late fifteenth-century work treating the story episodically, with the scene in the forest at the foot, and the martyrdom of the saint and his family in a brazen bull, with a fire sizzling below, at the top. At the summit of the painting angels are carrying the souls of the martyrs up to heaven.

As well as the intrinsic charm and interest of this painting showing characters dressed in late fifteenth-century costumes, this is also an indication of the way in which the Benedictine community continued the decoration of the fabric with fresh paintings, stained glass and stone carvings right down to the Dissolution of the priory in 1540. Here, as elsewhere, they had no inkling of the storm of iconoclasm that was to accompany the Reformation wherever the extreme Protestants gained power with their radical approach to the teaching

*Wall paintings of St Eustace's life in the north choir ambulatory.*

of religion and the ordering of public worship.

In the years before and after the Second World War, Professor E.W. Tristram was engaged in superintending the restoration of the wall paintings in the cathedral. He executed some splendid and imaginative reconstructions of medieval paintings both on wall surfaces and on wood which were then framed and placed near the originals to give some idea of their former splendour. These include a reconstruction of the mural of St Paul now hanging outside

St Anselm's Chapel, reconstructions of the tester of the Black Prince's tomb hanging opposite, and of the painting of the Coronation of the Virgin from the tomb of Henry IV in a similar position at the head of the steps on the north side of the Trinity Chapel. A painting of the Martyrdom of St Thomas now hangs in the Martyrdom Transept. Several of the episodes from the life of St Eustace hang on the choir screen opposite the mural painting. In the crypt Tristram restored a vanished Annunciation at the foot of the tomb of Cardinal Morton, as well as making some paintings of the murals in St Gabriel's Chapel.

## The North Ambulatory

In the years following the Restoration of Charles II many books and pictures glorifying his martyred father, King Charles I, were produced. One of these hangs on the wall of the north ambulatory of the choir. It is an oil painting which shows the King kneeling in prayer, his hands on his breast; his earthly crown falls on the ground but a heavenly one, jewelled, descends from above in a ray of light. The garter is worn over his royal robe and he holds in his hand a crown of thorns. In the background on the left is a representation of the cathedral as it was in 1660, standing on a rock to represent the indestructible Church of God, with a palm tree close by. This picture would have been painted soon after the Restoration of 1660 during the primacy of Archbishop Juxon who, as Bishop of London, had attended Charles I on the scaffold. It hung originally over the central doorway of the pulpitum screen but was later removed to the library. After the First World War it was placed in its present position and has recently been cleaned.

Two other pictures hang nearby on the wall of the north ambulatory. One is a very large picture of the murder of Thomas Becket and was the work of John Cross, a mid-Victorian painter, who was born in 1819 and died in 1861 at the age of 42, leaving his family impoverished. Some of his friends purchased this picture after his death to benefit the stricken family, and presented it to the cathedral as being the most appropriate place for it to hang. It had previously been exhibited at the Royal Academy in 1850 and later at the Royal College of Arts. On the wall below is an impression by the late Frank Salisbury of the visit of King George VI, Queen Elizabeth and Princess Elizabeth to the cathedral on 11 July 1946 to give thanks to God for the preservation of the cathedral from destruction in the Second World War. They are shown coming through the door of the pulpitum screen at the conclusion of the service of thanksgiving. Descending the steps below is an impressive procession of clergy in copes headed by the archbishop, Geoffrey Fisher, and the suffragan and assistant bishops of the diocese, all wearing mitres, escorted by Dean Hewlett Johnson and the canons of the cathedral Chapter.

Opposite is a lovely reproduction of two of the panels of the Tudor tapestry (see p. 00), once in the cathedral choir, and now at Aix en Provence. These show the Triumphal Entry into Jerusalem and Christ washing the disciples' feet and are the work of Noel Edwards (later Mrs Hewlett Johnson).

### St Martin's Chapel

In the Chapel of St Martin in the north-east transept are two sharply contrasted paintings. In a heavy frame with a crenellated top is a late medieval oil painting of the Saxon Queen Ediva, a great benefactress of the monks, whose relics were preserved here. She was the queen of King Edward, son of Alfred the Great. Her relics were placed here after the rebuilding of the eastern arm of the church following the great fire of 1174. On the wall are scratched the words *'Ediva Regina'*. This may have been one of a series of pictures painted during the fifteenth century representing persons who had played an important part in the affairs of the priory which were hung on the walls at great festivals to teach the illiterate about the history of the cathedral. The Queen is shown full-face, robed and crowned, with a seaside town behind, said to be Birchington, with several vessels out at sea. Trees and foliage appear as part of the background and in the wood stands a forester. The rhyming inscription below refers to the manors given by Ediva to the monks. They included Monkton, Meopham, Lenham and Osterland. Mr Woodruff thought that the words *'Joannes Pictor fecit'* referred not to the painter but to Prior John Oxney, who may have commissioned the picture and ruled the priory from 1468 to 1471.

Behind the altar here is an attractive triptych in the style of the Italian Primitives and suitably framed. It shows scenes from the life of St Martin of Tours including the famous incident with the beggar. The artist was Winifred Margaret Monnington, the first woman to win the Rome scholarship in 1920 as an inscription nearby records. She was born in 1899 and died in 1947.

Two late medieval paintings on wood, in curious curved frames, hang on either side of the Chapel of St Michael in the south-west transept. Much restored, they show St Gregory and St Augustine in monochrome and must date from the last quarter of the fifteenth century. There seems to have been an organ in a loft here in monastic times and these pictures may have covered the corbels on which the loft rested.

In 1951 several pictures of 'Old Masters' from the Cook collection were lent for exhibition in the cathedral and subsequently two of these were bought for the cathedral. One is a large sixteenth-century painting of St Christopher which hangs on a pillar at the west end of the nave. In the Middle Ages it was generally believed that those who saw a representation of this patron saint of travellers in church would travel safely on that day. Hence the prevalence of paintings of St Christopher near the main door in many medieval churches and cathedrals. This paintings comes from the Certosa at Ferrara and was originally a fresco painting on a wall of this Carthusian convent which was removed in 1844, and transferred to canvas and framed. The artist is Benvenuto Tisi (1481-1519) usually known as Garofano, the Italian name for a carnation, the flower with which he often 'signed' his paintings. The other picture hangs behind the altar of St John the Evangelist and is an 'Adoration of the Shepherds', the work of Bartolomeo Schidoni (1570-1615) of the school of Parma whose best known master was Corregio.

In St Gregory's Chapel, close by, is a charming modern icon of St Gregory and St Augustine of Canterbury. This was a gift from a group of monks from the Benedictine Abbey of Chevtogne in Belgium who stayed as guests of the Chapter for a week in 1984. This abbey is specially concerned with ecumenical relationships, particularly with the Orthodox Church.

## The Huguenot Chapel

There are two paintings in the Huguenot Church in the crypt. One appears to show a band of refugees in seventeenth-century costume ascending the cliffs above Dover Castle on their way to Canterbury, presumably fleeing from France after the Revocation of the Edict of Nantes in 1685 by Louis XIV. The painting is signed J. Johnson 1866 and is said to have been found in a public house in Dover. On the side of the organ, in the chapel, is a modern monochrome painting (perhaps taken from a photograph) of a statue of Admiral Gaspard de Coligny, the first victim of the Massacre on St Bartholomew's Day 1572.

## The Library

In the main cathedral library are some indifferent portraits of long dead ecclesiastics, of which only two have any artistic merit. One, of the school of Cornelius Janssen, is a portrait of Doctor Meric Casaubon, a most distinguished scholar and divine, who was Prebendary of the Ninth Stall from 1628 to 1671 when he was buried in the south-west transept. The other is a seated figure of the antiquarian clergyman, William Gostling, attributed to one of the Metz family of portrait painters in the latter part of the eighteenth century. Gostling died aged 82 in March 1771 after 50 years as a minor canon of the cathedral. His classic book, 'A Walk in and about the City of Canterbury' gives an unrivalled picture of the city and cathedral in the second half of the eighteenth century. Also preserved in the library is a curious fragment of a larger painting, thought to have been of the Scourging of Christ: it shows a torturer, with a three-tailed scourge, lashing a lost figure, presumbaly Our Lord. It is certainly late medieval in date, and Flemish or German in style and is said to have been found in the old Chequer Building which was demolished in 1868.

In one of the rooms of Eleven, the Precincts (the administrative headquarters of the Cathedral Chapter not usually open to the public), hangs a large picture attributed to Pieter de Neefs but more likely by one of his pupils. It shows the cathedral choir after the depredations of the Puritan fanatics, earlier in the seventeenth century, had been repaired and dates from about 1680. The two rows of monastic stalls are still in position but the parclose screen of Prior Eastry has disappeared behind a great insertion of wainscoting similar to that which can still be seen by the contemporary return stalls of the

*Graffiti in All Saints Chapel.*

Dean and Chapter at the west end. This was all inserted by Roger Davis, a joiner of London, in 1676 who was later to work under Wren on the stalls of St Paul's Cathedral. The new brass lectern, purchased in 1663, is in position facing south and a priest, in choir habit, is apparently reading the Bible for the benefit of passers by while other robed clergy sit, in rather a desultory fashion, in the stalls on each side of the choir. There is a very handsome altar piece and reredos in the ancient place, with rails in front, but no sign of a pulpit or throne for the archbishop. There seems to be a lot of stained glass in the windows, though this may be merely artistic licence, and in the south ambulatory is an iron grille with a crenellated crest along the top.

### Graffiti

All over the cathedral can be seen grafitti of various kinds, mostly masons' marks, dating from every century from the time of Ernulf, *c.* 1100 to the late fifteenth-century. The most impressive scratching, protected by glass, can be seen on the south-west wall of the eastern crypt behind the return stalls for the clergy. This shows Christ in Majesty seated among the symbols of the four Evangelists and dates from the early thirteenth century. Professor Tristram thought that this and other scratchings in the building were 'subjects incised in the stone, either as a preparation for paintings which have since perished, or, perhaps, at a later date over the remains of such paintings as were then still visible'. The eagle of St John appears in various places in the Trinity Chapel and, behind a buttress on the north side of the chapel, is a scratching showing Our Lord at the Last Supper with St John leaning his head on Christ's bosom. In the Chantry Chapel of Henry IV is a scratching recording the purchase of an image and its cost — 19 shillings and 11 pence — a 'doodle' which has survived to intrigue later generations.

### The Plate

An inventory of the furniture of the cathedral including plate, ornaments and vestments was made when the monastery was dissolved in 1540. This still survives and demonstrates the extraordinary wealth of altar plate for the use of the High Altar and the twenty or more side altars of the building. Within a few years almost all these treasures had vanished either through theft, misappropriation or legitimate sale for various purposes connected with the welfare of the Church.

*The Arundel Chalice (1636).*

What little survived from the Reformation must have finally disappeared under the Commonwealth. Today the best vessels and plate are those which were purchased after the Restoration for the necessary service of the Altar. Some of this vanished, one night in March 1968, when burglars raided the Romanesque Vestiarium and stole some valuable pieces of the Restoration period which have never been recovered. The generosity of Victorian canons and gifts in our own century have ensured that the cathedral is adequately equipped for the large congregations who communicate, not only on Festivals, but on ordinary Sundays throughout the year especially in the summer.

In July 1979 with the aid of a very generous subvention from the Goldsmiths' Company the Cathedral Chapter was able to furnish and open a treasury at the west end of the Norman crypt which houses many fine pieces of plate belonging to the cathedral and to the churches in the diocese and the archbishopric of Canterbury. This treasury is open, without charge, every weekday from 10.30 to 12.30 and from 2.30 to 4.30 between Easter Tuesday and All Saints' Day. Here will be seen two silver plates or ablution basins, dating from about 1400, made originally for the monastic foundation in Oxford known as Canterbury College. There are also two splendid silver pricket candlesticks, once thought to have been given by Cardinal Pole c. 1556, but more probably copies made at the Restoration. Two silver maces bearing the arms of the chapter and of the see of Canterbury to be carried by the vergers were also made especially at that time, together with a silver gilt flagon and two chalices bearing the chapter arms of 1665.

Two silver gilt patens of 1756 match the earlier chalices, the gift of Philip Weston of Bostock. A fine set of plate from Lambeth Palace consists of flagon, chalice, paten, alms dish, all silver gilt, with the emblem of the Paschal Lamb (a pun on Lambeth), dating from the first years of Charles II's reign. Perhaps the most impressive piece is a silver gilt chalice, thought to be Italian, given by Thomas Howard, Earl of Arundel and Surrey who visited Canterbury in 1636 on his way to the court of the Holy Roman Emperor as ambassador from Charles I. A simple verger's mace dated 1664 was the gift of Archbishop Sancroft 1678 to 1691 for the special use of the archdeacon of Canterbury, an office that he himself had once held. It is now borne ceremonially before the archdeacon when he holds his annual visitation and also when he preaches the annual sermon on Ascension Day in the cathedral, as well as when he goes as the representative of the archbishop to enthrone the bishops of the province of Canterbury in their cathedral churches. Of the same

*The Anglo-Saxon sundial.*

period is a Bible in a fine silver cover with the arms of the chapter on the front which was given by Dean Turner in thanksgiving for his return from exile at the Restoration 1660. Two silver communion cups 1631 to 1632 are on loan from the Huguenot Church.

In the case in the centre are some unusual treasures. One is a small Saxon sundial, sometimes known as St Dunstan's watch since it is at least a thousand years old and may well have belonged to this great monk Archbishop 960 to 988. It was discovered buried in the earth when the level of the cloister garden was lowered in 1938 and it is a tablet of silver with gold cap and chain having a pin or gnomon, with the names of months inscribed in pairs on the faces. Along the edges in Latin are the words *Pax Possessori* (God rest my owner) and *Salus Factori* (God bless my maker).

Other treasures came from the tomb of Archbishop Hubert Walter when it was opened in 1890. His crosier, in a special case, is a simple staff of cedar wood ornamented with some antique gems, whilst his episcopal ring is in the central case and has a green stone engraved with the emblem of the god, Chnuphis. Most precious are his silver

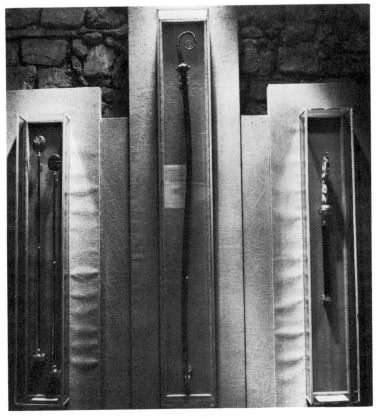

*Crosiers and maces from the crypt treasury.*

gilt paten engraved with the Agnus Dei, and a chalice of early thirteenth-century workmanship. This is, probably, the earliest example known of a Gothic paten and chalice. The pins with which the archbishop secured his pallium to his vestments are also silver gilt with delicate floral heads.

Victorian crosses and modern altar vessels belonging to the cathedral are also on display in this treasury with a set of medals given by Pope John Paul II on his visit to the cathedral in 1982. The use of copes and eucharistic vestments in the worship of the cathedral only dates back to 1931 but among the objects of historic interest are the mitre, stole, buskins, shoes and fragments of the vestments worn by Hubert Walter when celebrating pontifical high mass which are normally kept in the cathedral library. In the last years of the nineteenth century Dean Farrar had replicas made of the chasuble, dalmatic and tunicle used by St Thomas of Canterbury when in exile in Sens and still in the cathedral Treasury there. These replicas are worn by the sacred ministers in Canterbury on the feasts of St Thomas on 29 December and 7 July each year.

Many new frontals and eucharistic vestments have been acquired during the last decade for the enrichment of public worship in the cathedral. These include a fine set of festival copes for the Dean and Chapter designed by Beryl Dean and first used at the enthronement of Dr Donald Coggan in 1975.

### Books

Three different buildings house the very large collection of books and manuscripts belonging to the cathedral. All on the eastern side of the cloisters, they cluster near the north-east transept. At the end of the Middle Ages the monastic library was housed on an upper storey over the Prior's Chapel, erected by Archbishop Chichele, *c.* 1440, where unfortunately fire broke out in 1538 destroying many books. In the next half century some of the most ancient treasures, which had survived the fire and the subsequent dissolution of the monastery, were appropriated by Archbishops Parker and Whitgift as well as by Dean Nevil. They were given to the libraries of their respective colleges in Cambridge where they remain to this day.

The collection was further depleted in 1649 by the Puritans but a determined attempt was made in 1660 to build up a decent library again. Archbishop Juxon gave £500 to erect the red brick building alongside the north-east transept in place of the old Priors' Chapel and library above, which had been pulled down during the Commonwealth. This pleasant room had become too small for the increasing number of books acquired between 1660 and 1860, amounting to more than four thousand printed volumes and five thousand manuscripts. In 1868 a new building was erected on the site of the Great Dormitory of the priory adjoining the Chapter House. This was designed by the cathedral architect, H.G. Austin, who utilized the west wall of Lanfranc's Dormitory for his new building. Twenty years later the red brick building, erected by the munificence of Archbishop Juxon, was brought into use again to house the 12,500 volumes of the Howley-Harrison bequest, so called because it is made up of the library of Archbishop Howley, which he bequeathed to Archdeacon Benjamin Harrison, who had been his chaplain. He, in turn, bequeathed it to the cathedral, with his own considerable library added to that of his benefactor.

During the great raid on Canterbury, in the night of 1 June 1942, a high explosive bomb completely wrecked the library building of

1868 but, mercifully, no damage was done to the Howley-Harrison library and the damage to books generally was slight. Some years after the end of the war the Chapter decided to rebuild and in 1951 approved a design by the architect, John I. Denman, to be erected on the original site, again utilizing Lanfranc's west wall which had survived intact. This fine building was opened on 18 July 1954.

A final addition to the library complex was opened in 1966 thanks to a generous gift from the Wolfson Foundation. This consists of a wing at right angles to the Howley-Harrison Library, inserted into the remains of the old monastic Chequer Building demolished a hundred years before.

Among the many medieval manuscripts of great interest and importance are some thirty-three Anglo Saxon Charters going back as far as the year 742AD and more than seventy Anglo-Norman Charters. There are about two thousand five hundred account rolls of the medieval monastery and twenty-one bound volumes of monastic registers, as well as many registers of the post-Reformation Chapter. Particularly interesting is the Accord of Winchester, a deed signed (with crosses in lieu of names) by William the Conqueror and Matilda, his Queen. In this the primacy of Canterbury over York is agreed with signatures of both archbishops. Two deeds, witnessed by St Thomas Becket, as Chancellor, are also preserved in the library archives.

The library is open by appointment only every weekday from Monday to Friday, 9.30am to 12.45pm and 2pm to 4.30pm. The director is the archivist to the cathedral, diocese and city of Canterbury. In caring for the six thousand ancient charters and many other manuscripts the director is assisted by another trained archivist and a conservator as well as the Keeper of the Printed Books which amount to some fifty thousand volumes in all.

OPPOSITE: *The Howley-Harrison Library.*

# THE ARCHBISHOPS OF CANTERBURY

The exact number of archbishops is controversial. Some authorities omit Reginald FitzJocelyn who was elected in 1191 but died before consecration, and also John Ufford who was elected in 1349 but died of the Black Death before consecration. Some count Thomas Arundel twice over since he was deprived by Richard II and then restored by Henry IV, but this seems rather absurd.

| | | | |
|---|---|---|---|
| 597 | St Augustine | 1279 | John Peckham |
| 604 | St Laurentius | 1294 | Robert Winchelsey |
| 619 | St Mellitus | 1313 | Walter Reynolds |
| 624 | St Justus | 1328 | Simon Meopham |
| 627 | St Honorius | 1333 | John Stratford |
| 655 | St Deusdedit | 1349 | John Ufford |
| 668 | St Theodore of Tarsus | 1349 | Thomas Bradwardine |
| 693 | Berchtwald | 1349 | Simon Islip |
| 731 | St Tatwine | 1366 | Simon Langham |
| 735 | Nothelm | 1368 | William Whittlesey |
| 741 | Cuthbert | 1375 | Simon Sudbury |
| 759 | St Breogwine | 1381 | William Courtenay |
| 766 | Jaenberht | 1397 | Thomas Arundel |
| 793 | Aethelhard | 1398 | Roger Walden |
| 805 | Wulfred | 1399 | Thomas Arundel (restored) |
| 832 | Feologild | 1414 | Henry Chichele |
| 833 | Ceolnoth | 1443 | John Stafford |
| 870 | Aethelred | 1452 | John Kemp |
| 890 | Plegmund | 1454 | Thomas Bourchier |
| 914 | Athelm | 1486 | John Morton |
| 923 | Wulfhelm | 1501 | Henry Dean |
| 942 | St Odo | 1503 | William Warham |
| 960 | St Dunstan | 1533 | Thomas Cranmer |
| 988 | Ethelgar | 1556 | Reginald Pole |
| 990 | Sigeric | 1559 | Matthew Parker |
| 995 | Aelfric | 1576 | Edmund Grindal |
| 1005 | Aelfeah (St Alphege) | 1583 | John Whitgift |
| 1013 | Lyfing | 1604 | Richard Bancroft |
| 1020 | Aethelnoth | 1611 | George Abbot |
| 1038 | Eadsige | 1633 | William Laud |
| 1051 | Robert of Jumieges | | (vacancy after Laud's execution |
| 1052 | Stigand (deprived 1070) | | in 1645 until 1660) |
| 1070 | Lanfranc | 1660 | William Juxon |
| 1093 | St Anselm | 1663 | Gilbert Sheldon |
| 1114 | Ralph D'Escures | 1678 | William Sancroft (deprived 1690) |
| 1123 | William de Corbeuil | 1691 | John Tillotson |
| 1139 | Theobold | 1695 | Thomas Tenison |
| 1162 | St Thomas Becket | 1716 | William Wake |
| 1174 | Richard | 1737 | John Potter |
| 1185 | Baldwin | 1747 | Thomas Herring |
| 1193 | Reginald FitzJocelyn | 1757 | Matthew Hutton |
| 1193 | Hubert Walter | 1758 | Thomas Secker |
| 1207 | Stephen Langton | 1768 | Frederick Cornwallis |
| 1229 | Richard Grant | 1783 | John Moore |
| 1234 | St Edmund Rich | 1805 | Charles Manners-Sutton |
| 1245 | Boniface | 1828 | William Howley |
| 1273 | Robert Kilwardby | 1848 | John Bird Sumner |

1862 Charles Thomas Longley
1868 Archibald Campbell Tait
1883 Edward White Benson
1897 Frederick Temple
1903 Randall Thomas Davidson
1928 Cosmo Gordon Lang

1942 William Temple
1945 Geoffrey Francis Fisher
1961 Arthur Michael Ramsey
1974 Frederick Donald Coggan
1980 Robert Alexander Kennedy Runcie

## DEANS OF THE CATHEDRAL CHURCH

798 Cuba
805 Beornhead
813 Heahfrith
820 Ceolnoth
830 Aegelwyn
871 Eadmund
  ? Alfric
  ? Kensyn
930 Maurice I

930 Aelfwyn
935 Alsine
951 Aelfwyn II
  ? Athelsine
984 Aegelnoth
1026 Egelfric
1058 Goderic

(? exact date unknown)

## PRIORS OF THE CATHEDRAL

1080 Henry
1096 Ernulf
1108 Conrad
1126 Gosfrid
1128 Elmer
1137 Jeremy
1143 Walter Durdens
1149 Walter Parvus
1153 Wibert
1167 Odo
1175 Benedict
1177 Harlewine
1179 Alanus
1186 Honorius
1189 Roger Norris
1190 Osbern de Bristow
1191 Geoffrey
c. 1213 Walter III
1222 John de Sittingbourne
1232 John de Chatham
1234 Roger de Lee

1244 Nicholas de Sandwich
1258 Roger de St Alphege
1264 Adam de Chillenden
1274 Thomas Ringmere
1285 Henry de Eastry
1331 Richard Oxenden
1338 Robert Hathbrand
1370 Richard Gillingham
1376 Stephen Mongeham
1377 John Fynch
1391 Thomas Chillenden
1411 John Wodensburgh
1428 William Molash
1438 John Salisbury
1466 John Elham
1449 Thomas Goldstone I
1468 John Oxney
1471 William Petham
1472 William Sellinge
1495 Thomas Goldstone II
1517 Thomas Goldwell

# DEANS OF THE NEW FOUNDATION

1542 Nicholas Wotton
1567 Thomas Godwyn
1584 Richard Rogers
1597 Thomas Nevil
1615 Charles Fotherby
1619 John Boys
1625 Isaac Bargrave
1642 George Aglionby
1643 Thomas Turner
1672 John Tillotson
1689 John Sharp
1691 George Hooper
1704 George Stanhope
1728 Elias Sydall
1734 John Lynch
1760 William Friend
1766 John Potter
1770 Hon Brownlow North
1771 John Moore

1775 Hon James Cornwallis
1781 George Horne
1790 William Buller
1793 Folliott Herbert Walker Cornwall
1797 Thomas Powys
1809 Gerrard Andrewes
1825 Hon Hugh Percy
1827 Hon Richard Bagot
1845 William Rowe Lyall
1857 Henry Alford
1871 Robert Payne-Smith
1895 Frederick William Farrar
1903 Henry Wace
1924 George Kennedy Allen Bell
1929 Hugh Richard Lawrie Sheppard
1931 Hewlett Johnson
1963 Ian Hugh White-Thomson
1976 Victor Alexander de Waal

# Acknowledgements and Bibliography

More than sixty years ago, as a boy at the Junior Kings School I began my studies in the history and architecture of Canterbury Cathedral by buying a copy of Hartley Withers' book on the subject in Bell's *'Cathedral Series'*, following this up by purchasing, in due course, Woodruff and Danks *'Memorials of Canterbury Cathedral'*, published by Chapman and Hall in 1912 and S. Warner's book on the cathedral published in 1923 by S.P.C.K. In 1928 I joined the Friends of the Cathedral and began to read with avidity the regular publications of that body — invaluable Reports and Chronicles full of information about every possible aspect of the cathedral, its life and history. With these I included the annual volumes of *Archaeologia Cantiana*, the organ of the Kent Archaeological Society. When, some sixty years later I was invited by Bell and Hyman to be responsible for the text of a new guide to the cathedral I responded with alacrity for I knew very well that I should not be short of material.

I should like to express my gratitude to all who have helped with the production of this book, not least the Dean and Chapter of the cathedral and their staff which includes the vergers, Mr. Cole and Mrs. Lennox of the Stained Glass Restoration Workshop, Mr. Peter Marsh the Surveyor of the Fabric, Mr. Brian Lemar the Clerk of Works, and Miss Anne Oakley the Archivist, to mention only a few of them. It has been a pleasure to work with the editors of Bell and Hyman, to whose kindness and efficiency I am greatly indebted for keeping me up to the mark all along the line and, of course to Peter Burton and Harland Walshaw who have gone to endless pains to take the photographs which illuminate, so well, the text. Mr. Gareth Jones, at short notice, has supplied me with the plans of the cathedral and its crypt while without the help of my wife, who has not only typed my manuscript but also given me invaluable advice and encouragement on the text, the book would never have seen the light of day.

In addition to the sources quoted above I have been grateful for the information to be found in the following books:

AMONG THE STANDARD BOOKS ON THE CATHEDRAL

Willis, Professor R. *The Architectural History of Canterbury Cathedral* (Originally published in 1845, reprinted in 1972 by Paul P.B. Minet.)

Gostling, The Rev. William *A Walk in and about the City of Canterbury* 1825.

Somner, William *Antiquities of Canterbury,* Revised by Nicholas Batteley, 1703.

Republished with introduction by William Urry in 1977.


MODERN BOOKS CONSULTED INCLUDE

Babington, M. *Canterbury Cathedral* J.M. Dent, 1947.

Brooks, N. *The Early History of the Church of Canterbury* Leicester University Press, 1984.

Caviness M. *The Early Stained Glass of Canterbury Cathedral* Princeton University Press 1973.

Harvey J. *Henry Yevele* Batsford 1944. *English Mediaeval Architects* Batsford 1954.

Lang-Sims L. *Canterbury Cathedral* Cassell 1979.

Newman, John *The Buildings of England, North East and East Kent.* Pages 164-221. Penguin Books, 1969.

Rackham B. *The Ancient Glass of Canterbury Cathedral* Lund Humphries 1949.

Tristram E.W. *English Mediaeval Wall Painting* Volumes on the twelfth century in 1944 and volumes on the thirteenth century in 1950. Published for the Pilgrim Trust by O.U.P.

Woodman F. *Architectral History of Canterbury Cathedral* Routledge and Kegan Paul 1981.

*Mediaeval Art and Architecture at Canterbury before 1220*
British Archaeological Association Conference Transactions for 1979. Published jointly in 1982 with the Kent Archaeological Society.

While there have been many other books and articles, which have been helpful in the writing of this one, it is the experience of living under the shadow of the glorious Church of Christ in Canterbury for many years that has supplied the real inspiration and dynamic for the last twelve months of work. If the completed work and its fine illustrations, now offered to the public, help some of those who read it to fall in love with one of the most enthralling buildings ever erected for the worship of God, the Blessed Trinity, then it will amply have fulfilled the desires and intentions of its author.

DEREK INGRAM HILL

# Glossary

ALMUCE
A fur-lined cape worn over the surplice by canons and other clergy including members of some religious orders in medieval days; until recently still in use in some cathedrals in France.

AMBULATORY
A processional way or aisle very often encircling the apse of a cathedral.

BEEBOLES
Apertures in brick walls used in the past for storing straw skeps or hives for bees.

BUSKINS
Silken stockings worn by great prelates in the Middle Ages when celebrating High Mass pontifically.

CALEFACTORIUM
The warming house of a monastery.

CANOPY
A covering over a tomb usually 'sheltering' an effigy below.

CANTED
As applied to an arcade. A device for making a compartment or bay slope outwards to extend its breadth. At Canterbury a canted arcade incorporates the chapel of St Anselm in the south choir ambulatory.

CHANTRY
A foundation usually attached to an altar in a church or chapel which was endowed for the saying of masses or offices for the repose of the soul of some deceased person.

CHAPTER
Usually a collective name for a body of clergy serving a cathedral or the church of a religious community. The assembly hall where such bodies meet officially is known as the Chapter House.

CHASUBLE
The principal eucharistic vestment: a sleeveless cloak varying in colour according to the season of the liturgical year.

CHIMERE
A sleeveless gown of either black or red material worn by bishops over their rochets.

CLERESTORY
The upper storey of a church pierced with windows, either in the nave or choir.

CONSTITUTIONS OF CLARENDON
Enactments put forward by Henry II of England to regulate the relations between Church and State in matters of jurisdiction, at a Council at Clarendon in 1164. Becket's refusal to accept these began the controversy between him and Henry whicha finally led to his murder.

COPE
A sleeveless cloak, usually of silk worn over surplice or alb in processions and on festival occasions by both clergy and

laity.

**CROSIER**

The pastoral staff of a bishop shaped like a shepherd's crook.

**DALMATIC**

A tunic worn at High Mass by the Deacon or Gospeller and also worn by bishops in medieval times under the chasuble.

**EMBRASURE**

Small opening in the wall of a church, usually splayed on the inside.

**ENCAUSTIC**

A term applied to tiles of earthenware, which have been glazed and decorated, to be used as paving material.

**FERETORY**

The area of a church where the principal shrine containing relics is placed.

**GARB**

An archaic word for costume or dress.

**GNOMON**

The rod or pin of a sundial which shows the time by its shadow for taking the sun's meridian altitude.

**HAGIOSCOPE**

A squint or hole cut in a wall to allow a view of an altar in a church from places from where otherwise it could not be seen.

**INVESTITURES**

A controversy of the eleventh and early twelfth century which arose over the claim of secular princes to invest prelates with crosier and ring and to receive their homage before their consecration.

**JUPON**

A heraldic surcoat, often worn over armour on the battlefield or at tournaments.

**LAVATORIUM**

A washing place, usually in a monastic cloister.

**LIERNE**

A term used of vaulting. A lierne vault is one composed largely of ribs which do not spring from one of the main springers or from a central boss. It was introduced during the fourteenth century.

**LOZENGE**

A diamond shaped object, usually a heraldic shield.

**MANDORLA**

A halo or glory surrounding the figure of Our Lord or a Saint in Christian art, usually oval in shape and pointed at head and foot.

**MATTOCK**

A tool like a pickaxe but with two arms, one ending in an adze and the other an axe edge.

**MISERICORDS**

Choir stalls which have a bracket underneath the seat, usually carved with figures or designs.

**MITRE**

The ceremonial head dress of a bishop.

**MULLIONS**

Vertical uprights, usually of stone, dividing a window into sections or 'lights'.

**OBIT**

The office of the dead, especially a Requiem.

**PALLIUM**

A strip of white wool, shaped

like a Y, worn by archbishops in communion with Rome.

**PANTOCRATOR**
Title given to God as the Supreme Lord of All in Orthodox religious language.

**PARCLOSE**
A screen of wood or stone enclosing a chapel or choir.

**PATEN**
A small plate, usually of silver, on which the communion bread is placed for consecration.

**PENTISE**
A passage or alley, against a wall, covered by a sloping roof.

**PISCINA**
A basin with a drain by an altar for cleansing sacred vessels after Mass.

**PONTIFICALS**
The full vesture of a bishop when singing High Mass solemnly.

**POSTERN**
A side or back door of a building.

**PREDIEU**
A wooden desk at which prayer can be said kneeling.

**PRESBYTERY**
That part of the chancel of a church which lies between choir and altar.

**PRIORY**
A religious community ruled by a prior elected by the monks as their superior.

**PULPITUM**
A screen usually of stone in a cathedral or greater church separating the community in the choir from the lay folk in the nave.

**REBUS**
A punning device used in heraldry and medieval art as a play on a name.

**REREDOS**
A solid structure, very often carved and gilded, erected behind and above an altar.

**ROCHET**
A sleeveless surplice often worn by servers or musicians. A bishop's rochet has tight sleeves.

**SCREEN**
See pulpitum and parclose; in parish churches usually a wooden structure surmounted by a loft and rood or crucifix dividing the chancel from the nave.

**SCRIPTORIUM**
That part of the monastery devoted to writing, painting and illumination.

**SENESCHAL**
An official attached to a cathedral or monastic church as a steward.

**SHAFT**
A slender column usually attached to a pillar or pier.

**SOFFIT**
The underside of an arch.

**SPANDREL**
Triangular surface between two arches.

**SQUINT**
See Hagioscope.

**STOLE**
A long and narrow strip of material worn over alb or surplice for the administration of the Sacraments; its colour following that of the season or feast.

STRAINER
An arch or girder, usually of stone or wood, inserted to prevent the walls from leaning.

TESTER
A canopy over an altar or tomb. Also used of a sounding board over a pulpit.

TRIFORIUM
A gallery or wall passage, either arcaded or blank, usually facing nave and/or choir at the height of the roof and below the clerestory.

TUNICLE
A vestment worn by the subdeacon at High Mass and also on occasion by the principal servers.

VESTURER
At Canterbury the title of the head verger.

WAINSCOT
Wooden panelling fastened to a wall.

*A carved grotesque figure now on exhibition in the crypt.*

# INDEX

Bold numerals refer to captions